SONNY BLOCH'S

Cover Your Assets

H. I. Sonny Bloch and Jerome L. Hollingsworth, Esq.

A PERIGEE BOOK

This book is dedicated to the men and women of this world who need
to cover their assets, especially Pauline Betty Davis Bloch
and Hilda Milady Antonia Cabrera.

"Structuring Life Insurance Trusts to Avoid Estate Tax Inclusion under Section 2035," excerpted with permission from *The Journal of Taxation*, © 1985 Warren Gorham Lamont, a division of Research Institute of America, Inc., Boston, MA. All rights reserved.

Perigee Books
are published by
The Putnam Publishing Group
200 Madison Avenue
New York, NY 10016

Library of Congress Cataloging-in-Publication Data

Bloch, H. I. Sonny.
[Cover your assets]
Sonny Bloch's cover your assets / H. I. Sonny Bloch and Jerome L. Hollingsworth, Esq.
p.   cm.
ISBN 0-399-51778-2
1. Estate planning—United States—Popular works.
I. Hollingsworth, Jerome L.   II. Title.   III. Title: Cover your assets.
KF750.ZB55   1992   92-10939   CIP
346.7305'2—dc20
[347.30652]

Cover design by Mike McIver
Back cover photo © 1992 by Kenneth J. Austin

Cover photo © 1992 Hilda Milady Cabrera

Printed in the United States of America
1   2   3   4   5   6   7   8   9   10

This book is printed on acid-free paper.

Introduction to Estate Planning

ESTATE PLANNING IS oriented toward preventive legal services. The idea is similar to that of preventive medicine. It is better and less expensive to avoid getting ill than it is to treat an existing illness. In a similar way, it is better and less expensive to organize your affairs so that you will not need to go to court than it is to go to court and win.

Estate planning addresses two areas of your life. First, illness or an accident could render you unable to handle your own affairs. Second, we are all going to die eventually. If you do not provide your spouse or your family with authority to act on your behalf in the event of your incompetence, your spouse or your family must seek to be appointed as your guardian by means of a petition to the probate court. If you die without organizing your affairs properly, your spouse or your family must distribute the things you own under the supervision of the probate court. You can eliminate the necessity for any proceedings before the probate court by the stroke of a pen on the proper estate-planning documents.

The information which follows will give you the knowledge that you need to carry out these important goals. We are giving you the set of legal tools which you need to keep control of the things you own during your entire lifetime, to avoid the necessity for any probate proceedings, and to assure that everything you own is distributed as you wish after your death.

If the total value of everything you own is less than $600,000, you need not concern yourself with the Federal Gift and Estate Tax. Estate-planning lawyers refer to this as a small estate. If you have a small estate and have never been married, or if this is the first marriage for both you and your spouse, you will find what you need to know in chapters 1 through 9. You may still want to read Chapter 13 if you want to set some money aside for children.

Even though your estate is small, if this is a second marriage and you and your spouse do not treat all of each other's children·as though they were the children of this marriage, you should read Chapter 12.

If your estate is over $600,000, or if your estate could have a value of over $600,000 in the future, read every word! In the materials of chapters 10 through 15, we shall waltz you through the tax law and the schemes for avoiding the Federal Gift and Estate Tax.

The subjects covered in chapters 16 through 19 deal with special situations which may or may not apply to you. Our Lord never made two trees alike, let alone two families. Everyone's situation is different to one extent or another. If one of the special situations in these chapters applies to you, address the problem while you are alive and competent. Do not fear the future; provide for it. If you do not provide for the future, the state or someone else will do so for you. You may not like the provisions that they make.

We are not trying to teach you how to prepare your own estate-planning documents, although there is certainly no law against doing so. Seek the advice of an attorney who does estate planning. After reading the information we present to you, you will be in a position to evaluate the documents which your lawyer prepares. Share your thoughts with your lawyer and listen to any advice your lawyer gives you. Nobody has a monopoly on good ideas. Your lawyer may suggest something which you have not considered and which will help carry out your wishes.

Many, but not all, estate-planning attorneys will give you an initial consultation without charge. Ask about this when you make the appointment. Bring any deeds and your old will, if you have one. If you have made a list of your assets, bring that with you. An attorney can prepare an estate plan if you can state the type and approximate value of your assets and what you want done with your assets upon your death.

Some attorneys believe that you do not need an estate plan if you have very few assets. We disagree! A person with little money can even less afford the cost of a probate hearing to appoint a guardian or the cost of probate than someone with a great deal of money.

Find out what documents your attorney intends to prepare. Don't make this a test to find out whether your lawyer knows what he or she is doing, but be certain that after you sign your documents you will not need the services of an estate-planning attorney again.

Agree upon a price, or at least an approximate price, for the services which the lawyer will render. The law firm may be willing to arrange some sort of time payments if you cannot pay cash. If you have a small estate which consists of very little cash, the lawyer may reduce his fee to something you can afford to pay, or the law firm may have a special fee schedule for small estates.

The appendix contains a set of documents for a fictitious couple named Al and Betty Smith. Al and Betty are about forty-five years old and have three children, two of whom are minors. Their total estate consists of a home and some savings with a total value of about $200,000. They also own a survivor life-insurance policy with a death benefit of $300,000. These are the draft documents which an attorney would normally send to Al and Betty following the initial interview.

The letter in the appendix (pages 103–108) which explains the draft documents specifies all of the documents which you need if you want to avoid returning to your lawyer or going into the probate court. It would take a very unusual event or a change in the size of your estate for you to need the services of an attorney in the future once you have organized your affairs in this manner.

Although this is a small estate with a joint trust, the documents are essentially the same as those for a single or a split estate. Split-estate trusts contain an article which divides the trust into separate shares, or trusts, and the split estate would include a property agreement.

Contents

CHAPTER 1

The Basic Tools of Estate Planning

EVERYONE KNOWS SOMETHING about the law, and everyone knows something about what has come to be known as "estate planning." If we tell you something you already know, it should not offend you. Hopefully, we shall tell you many things you do not already know. Since we do not know what you already know, we shall be rather basic. The first time we use a term with a specific legal meaning, we shall put it in *italics*.

Lawyers refer to anything which someone can own as *property*. Your car, your furniture, your bank account, and the land you own is all property. At one time, only land was thought to have value. For this reason, land is known as *real property* or *real estate*. If you look at the deed to your home, you will notice that it conveys the *land* to you, but it does not mention that there is a house on the land. The house, the driveway, the lawn, and so forth are known as *improvements* to the land. All land is registered or recorded in the owner's name.

All property, other than land, is known as *personal property*. There are two types of personal property: *tangible personal property* and *intangible personal property*. Tangible personal property is something you can touch, such as your dishes. Intangible personal property is something you cannot touch, such as your bank account. (You may be able to touch the statement the bank sends you, but you cannot touch the account itself.) Intangible personal property, and some tangible personal property, is registered in the owner's name. Most tangible personal property is not.

Your dishes are not registered in your name, but you are the only person on the face of the earth to have *possession* of them. This shows that you are the owner. If you wish to change the ownership of this type of property, you simply change possession of the property. You *deliver* the dishes to the person to whom you have sold or given them. Sometimes delivery is not practical. Sometimes you may want to evidence the gift or the sale. You can do a symbolic delivery by signing a *deed of gift* or a *bill of sale*.

In summary, you can change the ownership of tangible personal property simply by changing possession of the property. However, if you own property which is registered or recorded in your name, you must sign some sort of document to accomplish a transfer of ownership. You sign the back of the title to your automobile or sign a deed conveying your land.

We are all going to die. Of course, if we were never going to die, we could never retire. When you are no longer living, all of your property will belong to someone else. Most of us want to name who will own our property after we are gone. We may also want to determine the circumstances under which the property will pass and be managed. In order to do this, you must state what your wishes are and provide a mechanism by which someone can carry them out. How can we transfer ownership of property when we are no longer living? When we are no longer living we can neither make deliveries nor sign papers. The law has provided us with four basic tools which we can use to do all of this.

You can avoid the entire problem by giving away everything you own and not owning anything when you die. There is an ancient Hebrew saying that sums that idea up pretty well: "Woe to the man who gives his property to his sons during his lifetime, for he becomes their servant." (At that time, he would have expected his daughters to get their property from someone else's sons.) Keep control of your property until the day you die! Stay as independent as you can.

The Last Will and Testament is the basic estate-planning tool. In a properly executed will, you can tell what you want done with your property and you can name the person who will carry out your wishes. Chapter 2 explains the history and present status of this tool.

Joint Ownership with Right of Survivorship is a second tool with which to pass ownership upon death. If someone were to put a car into joint ownership with you and then die, you would become the owner *by operation of law* upon the event of that person's death. That person's interest would be extinguished and yours would continue to exist. Chapter 4 is devoted to a discussion of this option.

Payable Upon Death is the mechanism by which contracts with a death benefit normally specify the beneficiary. Life insurance, IRA accounts, and many pension plans have a death benefit. In recent years, you have been able to make checking and savings accounts payable on death to someone by naming that person on the signature card. Chapter 5 discusses the problems involved.

The Living Trust has become the prime tool of estate planning today. You will see the many reasons for this as you read on. You will see that a living trust is nothing more than a different way of owning your property. You will hold title to everything as trustee for your own benefit and use. The result will be that you have already probated your will while you are living and you can make changes to that will anytime you wish. Nobody but your family will ever know what you own or what you did with it.

Many years ago, a fellow met the lawyer of a wealthy man, who had just died, and asked him, "How much money did old R.G. leave?" R.G.'s lawyer looked up and then down the street as if to assure privacy and said, "He left 'er all!" Like many wealthy people of the time, R.G. had a living trust and nobody ever found how much R.G. left.

CHAPTER 2

The Last Will and Testament

THE LAST WILL and testament in its present form is rather recent. By that we mean, it did not exist six or seven hundred years ago. Words such as "will" and "shall" have changed meaning in recent times. The word "will" expressed a wish, and "shall" was a word of command. You can understand the ancient meaning of these words through an ancient expression:

> "If you *will not* when you *may,* you *shall not* when you *will,* sir!" (emphasis added—author unknown)

In ancient times, a person would summon a priest and express his or her wishes in *testimony* to the priest in anticipation of death. The priest would write the wishes of the *testator* (male) or *testatrix* (female) as the *last will and testament* of that person. These wills often included a generous gift to the church. At that time, the church not only had the exclusive power to dispense the grace of God, but it also had its own courts, which carried out the distributions under the terms of the will.

As time went on, people tended to have lawyers prepare their wills. Eventually, the civil courts held jurisdiction over matters concerning wills. The first step after the death of the testator or testatrix was the *probate* of the will. Probate is the name given to the court proceeding in which the judge makes a determination that the document before the court is truly the last will and testament of the deceased person. Lawyers began to add formalities to the will to make it easier to prove the will's validity.

The testator or testatrix *declares* to witnesses that the document before him or her expresses his or her wishes. The testator or testatrix then either signs the document before the witnesses or points to the signature or mark and declares that it was his or her signature or mark. The witnesses then sign in the presence of the testator or testatrix and in the presence of each other. At the time of probate, the witnesses tell what happened.

Whenever you do something which the law considers to be important, the law will require you to do it with certain formalities. The formalities may require the use of witnesses or a notary public. Different legal documents require different formalities in order to be effective, and the requirements are different in different states. Generally speaking, a legal document is effective if it meets the legal requirements of the state in which it is executed, at the time it is executed.

State legislatures have enacted statutes which specify the required formalities for a will. Most states require two witnesses to a will, and many require that neither of the witnesses has any interest in the estate of the person who is making the will.

One of the ways in which someone can contest a will is to allege that it was not properly witnessed. In such a case, the person who is defending the will calls the witnesses to testify in court. However, sometimes the witnesses are not available to testify. Perhaps they are no longer living or perhaps we simply cannot find them.

Lawyers have devised a means by which it will not be necessary to call the witnesses to a will into court. This is called a *Proof of Will*. The witnesses and the person making the will go before a notary public and swear to the testimony which they would give in court. The notary public then signs a statement that the person making the will declared that it was made by free will and deed and that the person making the will and the witnesses executed the will in the presence of each other. The proof of will is usually in a form similar to the following:

PROOF OF LAST WILL AND TESTAMENT
We, Henry J. Schmidlap, Olga B. Barfarkel, and Fred M. Smith, the Testator and the witnesses, respectively, whose names are signed to the

foregoing instrument, having been sworn, declared to the undersigned officer that the Testator, in the presence of witnesses, signed the instrument as his Last Will and Testament, that the Testator signed for himself, and that each of the witnesses, in the presence of the Testator and in the presence of each other, signed the Will as a witness.

The testator or testatrix names someone in the will to carry out the plan of distribution specified in the will. In the past, this person was called the *executor* or *executrix*. A person with no will had an *administrator* or an *administratrix*. A gift of land in a will was called a *devise*, and a gift of personal property was called a *legacy*. The person to whom the land was given was called a *devisee*, and the person to whom personal property was given was called a *legatee*. The persons who will receive property upon the death of someone who dies without making a will are called *heirs*. The person from whom the heirs *inherit* is their *ancestor*.

Lawyers, judges, and everybody else have often used these terms incorrectly. Modern probate law has simplified the terminology a great deal. A person who carries out the wishes of the deceased is called a *personal representative*, and any gift made in a will is called a *devise*. The person to whom the deceased makes a devise is the *devisee*. Since everybody seemed to understand the terms testator and testatrix, we still use them. Likewise, a person who dies leaving a will is still said to have died *testate*, and a person who dies without a will is still said to have died *intestate*.

Anyone who has *testamentary capacity* can make a will. This capacity consists of three things:

1. *A person must know the nature and extent of his property.* It may surprise you that people sometimes have no recollection of what they own. These people do not have the capacity to make a will, because they do not know what they would be giving away.

2. *A person must know who are the natural objects of his gifts.* A person would normally leave his property to his spouse and children. Although a person can leave his property to whomever he wants, he cannot make a will if he does not know that he actually has a spouse or children.

3. *A person must understand his plan of distribution.* It doesn't matter whether the plan is simple or complex. The testator or testatrix must be able to articulate the plan without prompting. This is to ensure that someone else's plan is not contained in the will.

As you can see, a person could think himself to be Napoleon and still have the capacity to make a will. It sometimes happens. On the other hand, a person can be completely functional in the world and lack the testamentary capacity to make a will. There was a fellow in his nineties who drove his car, kept his own home, and who lived very frugally because he thought himself to be very poor. Nobody was able to make him understand that he had several hundred thousand dollars in the bank.

Sometimes people who make wills change their minds. If you change your mind after making a will, you have three choices. First, you can destroy the old will and die intestate. Second, you can make a new will. Third, you can make a *codicil* which changes part of the old will. A codicil is an amendment to a will and must be executed with the same formalities as a will. Simply writing on the old will doesn't work.

When a person dies intestate, the *Law of Intestate Succession* determines the distribution of the property. This law varies from state to state, but there are some general rules. If someone dies with a spouse and no children, everything goes to the spouse. If someone dies without a spouse but with children, everything goes to the children. If someone dies with a spouse and children, the distribution will depend upon whether or not the children are also the children of the spouse. If there is no spouse and no children, the property goes to the parents and then to brothers and sisters of the deceased. The children of the surviving spouse in a second marriage and the family of the surviving spouse in a marriage without children often do very well when there is no will.

The Uniform Probate Code which the National Conference of Commissioners on Uniform State Laws has proposed provides for a *holographic*, or handwritten, will. In states where such a will is valid, it must satisfy three requirements. First, the will must be dated. Second, the operative provisions must be in the handwriting of the testator or testatrix. Third, the will must be signed at the end by the testator or testatrix. Anything which the testator or testatrix writes after the signature is void.

If a will does not dispose of all of the property of the deceased, the remainder of the property is distributed in accordance with the Law of Intestate Succession of the state where the will is probated. This situation most often arises in the case of a handwritten will. Lawyers use a checklist to avoid this problem.

Most wills contain a provision which directs the personal representative to pay the debts of the deceased. In the past, lawyers used language telling the personal representative to pay "the just debts" of the deceased. However, there have been cases where a probate court has ordered the personal representative to pay a debt because it would be "just" to do so, even though the statute of limitations had run out on the debt and the creditor could not enforce it. If the deceased had wanted to pay the debt, he could have done so during his lifetime. Most lawyers now use the words "legally enforceable debts" to avoid the situation where the court orders the personal representative to do something which the deceased would not want done.

You can make a *specific devise* in your will. For example, you can give your sewing kit to Uncle Henry. Many states have a statute that permits a person to make a separate list of specific devises which the testator or testatrix refers to in his or her will. If you can use such a list rather than listing the specific devises in your will, you can buy something which you want to leave to a specific person, add the item to your list, and not have to go back to your lawyer to make a new will. This is a very important part of your planning. We all know of families where brothers and sisters no longer talk to each other because mother promised the same brass bed to more than one of her children.

It is a good idea to tell your children that you are making a will. Ask them which items of your tangible personal property they would like. Explain to them that they will not receive the property for many years, but that you will put it on your list. When you are done, send each of them a copy of the list. In this way, you will remember to whom you promised to leave that lovely brass bed.

The next section of your will should contain a provision that disposes of the tangible personal property which you did not devise specifically in your will or on your list. Married couples usually give everything to each other and divide the property among the children according to their preferences upon the death of the second spouse to die. If there are things that nobody wants, they can be sold and the proceeds become part of the *residue* of the estate.

The residue of the estate is everything which is left after the specific devises and the distribution of the tangible personal property. The language which lawyers usually use is "the rest, residue, and remainder of my estate." This provision disposes of the stocks, bonds, land, and money which is left. Here again, married couples generally leave everything to each other and direct that it be divided equally among their children upon the death of both spouses. The normal distribution to the children is *per stirpes*. This means *by right of representation*. A deceased child's share goes to the deceased child's children.

A per stirpes distribution bypasses the spouse of a deceased child. If the child is in his or her twenties, such a distribution may be appropriate. We would hope that the child's spouse will remarry. However, if the child is in his or her sixties and the grandchildren are making more money than we ever hoped to make, the child is probably more concerned with his or her spouse than with the grandchildren. You can always make a specific devise of money to each of the grandchildren.

When two people are killed in a common disaster, such as a plane crash, it is often impossible to tell which one died first. The answer can be important if it determines who inherits under the terms of a will. For this reason, we put a provision in a will such as the following:

> If any beneficiary under this Last Will and Testament and I should die under circumstances as would render it doubtful whether the beneficiary or I died first, then it shall be conclusively presumed for the purposes of this, my Last Will and Testament, that I survived the beneficiary.

We put such a provision in a will to ensure that our plan of distribution and not someone else's plan is carried out. For example, if the child predeceased you, his or her share would go to your grandchildren. If the child survived you, he or she would receive his or her share and it would go to his or her spouse under the terms of his or her will.

Remember, a will has no legal effect whatsoever until the following two things happen:

1. You have to die. A will is said to be *ambulatory*; it walks as long as you walk. You can make a new will while you are still alive and as long as you have testamentary capacity.
2. Someone must take the will before the probate court to get the authority to carry out its provisions.

There are many people who think that they can avoid probate by making a properly executed last will and testament. Making a will ensures that your property will be distributed in accordance with your wishes. The state has made a will for anyone who does not make one for himself or herself. The Law of Intestate Succession is the will which the state has made for its citizens who do not choose to make their own wills.

If you wish to avoid probate, you must use a probate-avoidance device of some sort. The living trust is the most effective probate-avoidance device available. You will see that a living trust is actually a will which was already probated by the person or people who set up the trust.

You will find samples of a Last Will and Testament in the appendix beginning at page 127 and page 131. The explanation of the various items in the wills is on pages 106 and 107, pages 4 and 5 of the letter explaining the estate-planning documents. These are *pourover* wills. An ordinary will would have a different Item V. It would make a final disposition of the "rest, residue, and remainder" of the estate.

There is a Proof of Will after the signature of the testator or testatrix and the witnesses. There is no way to overemphasize the importance of this part of the will. For example, if an Indiana resident dies owning land in Florida and the land is not in a living trust, the will must go before the Florida probate court. Unfortunately the witnesses are in Indiana. We do not have to call the witnesses before the court if there is a proof of will, for the witnesses and the testator or testatrix have already testified before a notary.

CHAPTER 3

The Probate Court

OVER THE YEARS the probate courts, the probate judges, and the probate lawyers have incurred the hatred of the American public. Every family has a probate horror story they can tell you about a probate which took forever to complete and how the lawyers got all the money.

At present, the wealthiest lawyers practice in the field of personal injury and wrongful death. Prior to the time of large liability insurance policies, this was not the case. The wealthy attorneys were those who handled the probate of large estates. In most cases, they took a percentage of the estate rather than charging a fee for what they did. The courts have done much to simplify probate procedures in recent years. However, if you can avoid probate altogether, you are better off. Stay away from people sitting on elevated benches wearing black robes.

Probate begins with a *petition* to the probate court asking that the decedent's will be *admitted to probate*. The court reviews the will, perhaps takes testimony at a hearing in open court, and decides whether or not the will is valid under the laws of the state in which the probate is taking place. It is at this point that a will contest can occur. There are several grounds on which someone can challenge a will.

An heir could claim that the will was the result of *undue influence*. Perhaps the heir would have received more if there were no will and now wants to set the will aside.

If the deceased had called his own lawyer and only he and the lawyer were present at the meeting where he specified the distribution, the court will almost automatically state that there was no undue influence. The court begins with a presumption that the will is valid. If the distribution went to family members, undue influence is almost impossible to establish. However, if the old boy left everything to his housekeeper after she called her lawyer and was present at the meeting with the lawyer, the case could well be different. Right or wrong, the courts have had a very strong inclination to take care of the widows and the orphans.

Another claim is that of the *pretermitted heir*. This is a person who would normally be included in the distribution scheme but was not even mentioned in the will. The claim is that he was *inadvertently omitted*. If someone makes a will and then has a child after making the will, the child will not be mentioned unless there is a new will or a codicil. Sometimes parents mistakenly believe that one of their children is dead. When the child presents himself before the probate court, he would claim that he is a pretermitted heir. A pretermitted heir is normally awarded the share which he would have received if the deceased had died intestate.

The most interesting type of claim is where someone states that the deceased person made some sort of contract to leave him property. There are many examples of situations where a couple moved onto the farm, ran the farm operation, and took care of the old fellow until his death under an agreement with him that he would leave the farm to them.

After the will has been admitted to probate or the court has decided that the deceased died intestate, the court issues a document to the personal representative which is variously known as *letters of authority* or *letters of administration*. This is the document which gives authority to the personal representative to make the deliveries of tangible personal property and sign the conveyances of the property which was registered in the deceased's name. However, the personal representative must pay the legally enforceable debts of the deceased before making all of the distributions.

The personal representative will know of many of the debts which the deceased incurred before his death. In order to be certain that all of the debts are paid, the personal representative puts an advertisement in the paper of general circulation in the area. The ad says that if the deceased owed anyone money, that person is to contact the personal representative. Normally, the personal representative does not quibble about small amounts. It is too expensive in terms of attorney fees to do so. There have been scams where someone would watch for these ads, send a false bill to the personal representative for something or other, and receive payment.

After the personal representative has paid all the bills and filed such tax returns as may be necessary, the personal representative submits an accounting to the probate court and asks for an order to distribute the estate to the devisees or the heirs. When the court has issued the order, the personal representative makes the distribution.

Probate has become much faster and easier than it was in days gone by. It may also have become somewhat less expensive than it was in the past. However, if you organize your affairs properly, there will be no necessity to probate your estate, and all of your property will go to your family without any court proceedings whatsoever.

CHAPTER 4

Joint Ownership With Right of Survivorship

NEVER PUT ANYTHING you own, under any circumstances whatsoever, into joint ownership with anyone on the face of this earth, other than your spouse. If joint ownership between spouses is a problem, they have much larger problems than that property.

There are far more joint ownership horror stories than there are probate horror stories. As an estate-planning device it is very poor. In order for it to work, everyone has to die in the proper order. Sometimes people just don't want to die on time in order to carry out the scheme.

When you place property into joint ownership, you make a gift of part of the property. For example, grandmother bought a commercial parcel of land in the 1920s for $4,000 and operated a store on it for many years. When grandmother was eighty-nine years old, she decided that she wanted her granddaughter to receive the property when she died. She put it into joint ownership with her granddaughter. Upon grandmother's death, granddaughter sold the property for

$80,000 and paid about $20,000 in income tax on the gain between the selling price and the price grandmother paid. If grandmother had given the property to granddaughter through her will or living trust, granddaughter's *basis* in the property, or her cost of the property, would have been its fair market value at the time of grandmother's death. Under these circumstances, she would have had no gain at the time of the sale and would have paid no tax.

When you place property into joint ownership, you lose control of the property as well as part of the ownership. For example, grand-father is deceased and grandmother is living in East Overshoe, New Hampshire. She has some things in joint ownership with her children and some things in joint ownership with her grandchildren. It is winter and she realizes that while she is in New Hampshire with her feet wet and cold, her girlfriends are playing bridge by the pool in Naples, Florida. She decides to sell her GM stock and buy a condo in Naples.

This is the stock which grandmother put into joint ownership with her granddaughter about a year before her granddaughter's marriage. She tells her granddaughter of her plans and asks her to stop by and go with her to sell the stock. Granddaughter talks the matter over with her new husband, and he says, "I'll tell you what the ol' lady is going to do. She's going to sell the stock and then die. Your brother will get his, your aunt will get hers, your uncle will get his, and you'll get nothing. If you're so stupid as to sell that stock, I'm walkin' out the door!" Granddaughter goes to see her grandmother and says, "Grandmother, we talked it over, and . . ."

It's not usually your children who cause the problems. It's the people they marry. Wait until you meet your daughter's second hus-band. He's the one she married after her first husband got run over by a cement truck. It is a tragedy when grandmother gets her heart broken and cannot pay for the things she wants. Joint ownership has led to results far worse than that.

Father purchased an abandoned farm so that he and mother could live in the farmhouse and father could shoot an occasional pheasant. The barns and outbuildings stood idle, and father leased the pasture-land to others.

Son returned home from the army and announced that he wanted to become a dairy farmer. Father suggested that the young lad go ahead and do it and pointed out that the buildings were all there. Son worked hard, married, had children, built a beautiful home on the land, and prospered a great deal at farming. Father and son put the land into joint ownership so that son would get title to the farm when father died. Father continued to live in the old farm house.

At the age of fifty-five, son suffered a heart attack and died. He left a wife and two minor children. Mother was deceased and father was in failing health at the time of son's death. As a result of the joint ownership, the farm became father's sole property. Son's wife did not even own the home which she and her husband had built upon the land. Father's new wife did not want the farm to go to son's wife. She wanted it to go to her children.

If a married couple hold everything in joint ownership, all of the property will go to the surviving spouse upon the death of one of them. There will be no probate upon the occasion of this first death because the property will pass automatically, by operation of law. There will have to be a probate upon the death of the second spouse. Of course, if the two of them step out in front of the same cement truck at the same time, we will have to probate two estates instead of one.

CHAPTER 5

Payable on Death

THE SERIES E bonds issued during and since World War II could be made *payable on death* to an individual other than the one who bought the bond. The personal representative of one probate estate brought a six-inch-tall stack of these bonds into the attorney's office as part of the estate. All of them were payable on death to people who were already dead. The probate-avoidance scheme had failed.

Making an individual the death beneficiary of bonds, bank accounts, or life insurance proceeds creates one problem we encounter in joint ownership. Individuals die, and they don't necessarily do it at the right time.

By now, you can see that we don't favor any probate-avoidance scheme which requires people to die at the right time. Joint ownership can have some very unusual results. A ninety-two-year-old client inherited a great deal of money from her only daughter as the result of her daughter's untimely death and everything in joint ownership. This lady was well over four feet tall and in perfect health, except for her hearing. The attorney would get a headache from yelling at her during conversations when she would come to his office. From time to time

Sonny Bloch's Cover Your Assets

she would decide that she was going to "spend it all." The attorney told her that he didn't think she could do it. It was during one of her visits when she was ninety-five years old that he suggested that she buy a new Cadillac. She gave him a dirty look. The state had taken her driver's license away a week before, and she was as mad as a wet hen.

One of the reasons people use schemes of joint ownership and payable-on-death provisions is that they believe that they can devise a probate-avoidance scheme without the assistance of an attorney in this manner. If you are the sort of person who drills his own teeth and takes out his own appendix, you might feel very comfortable creating your own probate-avoidance scheme. These schemes often work. However, you have no assurance that your wishes for the distribution of your property will be carried out. It would be impossible to list all of the things which can go wrong.

One of the advantages of payable-on-death provisions over joint ownership is that you can often change the death beneficiary. This is not always true with life insurance. It depends on the terms of the policy.

Pages 171 and 172 which are pages 3 and 4 of the letter explaining how to transfer property into a living trust, show some uses of the payable-on-death provision. A person who has a living trust fills out a new signature card at the bank which makes the checking and savings accounts payable on death to the *successor trustee* of the living trust. In a similar manner, you make the successor trustee the death beneficiary of life insurance policies. You can handle an IRA or the death benefits from a pension plan in a similar manner. However, if you are married and rather young, you may want to make your spouse the death beneficiary so that he or she may roll the benefits over into his or her IRA and postpone the tax. The alternate beneficiary of an IRA or pension plan should still be the successor trustee of your living trust.

CHAPTER 6

The Living Trust

THE TRUST BEGAN as a tax-avoidance scheme. Lord Fuddlebottom would convey all of his property to his attorneys but reserve the use of the property to himself and his heirs. This meant that although he did not hold title to any property, he still had the benefit of it all. When Lord Fuddlebottom died and the king's tax collector came by to collect the inheritance tax, there was none to pay. Since Lord Fuddlebottom "owned" nothing, nothing passed to young Lord Fuddlebottom by inheritance.

Well, we all know the king would not let this go on for long. The *Statute of Uses* was the result. This statute stated that all title reverted to the person who held the use of the property. It did not occur to anyone to tax the passing of the *beneficial title* to the property. Finally, the Statute of Uses was repealed and the crown taxed the passing of the use.

For centuries the wealthy have held and administered their property through the use of a living trust. This mechanism has now come into common use by the population in general. One reason for this is the advent of computerized word processing in preparing documents.

A legal assistant or secretary can do in a day what would have taken a week with a typewriter.

A trust is an *agreement* or *contract* between a *settlor*, the person who *settles* or sets up the trust, and a *trustee*, the person or bank who is to administer the trust. The way in which a trust functions is very simple.

The settlor puts the title to all of the trust property in the name of the trustee, and the trustee does whatever the trust agreement says. The settlor does not lose control of the property, for the trust agreement gives him or her the right to change trustees, amend the terms of the trust agreement, or withdraw the property from the trust any time he or she wishes.

Today it is very common for a person to be his or her own trustee during lifetime, with some individual or a bank named as successor trustee. In a situation where there is a married couple and no exposure to the Federal Gift and Estate Tax, we often draft a joint trust. The couple may be their own joint trustees, or one of them can act as trustee. In the situation where there are joint trustees, the survivor becomes the sole trustee upon the death of one of them. Then, upon the death of the second, the successor trustee assumes the duties of the trustee and carries out the terms of the trust agreement. When there is only one trustee, the successor trustee takes over upon his or her death.

The successor trustee steps into the shoes of the original trustee or trustees. Since the successor trustee holds legal title to the property, the plan of management and final distribution specified in the trust agreement can proceed without the probate court. Furthermore, the scheme of distribution will work no matter in what order the people may die.

Most trusts contain a provision which presumes that in the event of a simultaneous death, all beneficiaries, other than a spouse, have predeceased the settlor in the event of a common disaster (page 122, Article XXI).

Even though you have a living trust, you still need a will. The day before you stepped in front of the cement truck, you won a million-dollar lottery prize. We create a *pourover will* which leaves the rest, residue, and remainder to your living trust. Since the trust contains your scheme of distribution, we want everything which is to be distributed to go into the trust upon your death. This is why you make checking and savings accounts, life insurance policies, IRA death benefits, and so forth payable on death to your living trust, unless your spouse is young enough to want to roll over IRA or pension benefits into an IRA.

It is possible to create a trust through a Last Will and Testament. The will contains the terms of the trust and generally names a trustee. This is called a *testamentary trust.*

The probate proceeding for a will containing a testamentary trust is far more complicated and expensive than the probate proceeding for an ordinary will. The probate court appoints the trustee, and the personal representative of the deceased transfers the property to the trustee rather than directly to the beneficiaries. In many cases, the trustee must report to the probate court annually, and often must seek specific permission from the court to pay money for the benefit of the persons for whom the trust was created. Court proceedings cost money which could go to beneficiaries. The attorney fees for preparing a will containing a testamentary trust and the fees for creating a living trust and a pourover will are about equal. A will creating a testamentary trust is almost as poor a method of estate planning as an ordinary will without a trust.

The simultaneous death provision in a pourover will is usually the opposite of this provision in an ordinary will. A pourover will usually dispose of nothing other than tangible personal property. Rather often, we want things which contain the family name to descend down the male side of the family and objects such as jewelry to descend down the female side of the family even in the event of an untimely death. For this reason, the pourover will contains the provision to the effect that in the event of a simultaneous death, all beneficiaries under the will have survived the testator.

The living trust is a contract, and all well-drafted contracts provide for events which we hope will never occur. However, if something occurs which is not covered by the contract, you may end up in court.

People create living trusts not to win when they get to court, but to avoid going to court at all. A properly drawn living trust contains a provision which states that if the trustee is, in the opinion of two physicians, unable to handle his or her affairs, the successor trustee will step into the shoes of the trustee (page 112, Article VI).

Likewise, the trust provides that the trustee *may* provide money to the personal representative of the settlor's estate to pay bills. The personal representative of the estate normally pays all legally enforceable debts, but if you do things properly, there will be nothing to probate. When the attorney uses the word "may," the trustee is not obligated to pay bills and nobody can make a claim against the trust for

31

debts. On the other hand, the trustee has the power to pay proper debts (page 111, Article V).

The trust should contain a provision stating that any person acting as trustee can appoint a *corporate trustee* as a substitute trustee. This could be a trust company or the trust department of a bank. Some stock brokerage houses also have a trust company. No individual wants to manage property for children. The statute of limitations on any child's claim against the trustee does not even start to run until the child reaches the age of eighteen years. Two years later, the child's new spouse says, "If that uncle of yours had done what he should have, you'd be a millionaire today!" (page 115, Article XI).

Any corporate trustee wants to have the right to resign. In any business there are customers you do not want. If the beneficiaries are a real problem, the corporate trustee will resign (page 120, Article XVI).

The trust should contain a provision under which the beneficiaries can change trustees. It may be that they think that a corporate trustee is unresponsive or is not doing a proper job with the investments (page 121, Article XVIII).

It is possible that the amount of property in the trust is simply too small to warrant investment. The trustee should have the power to terminate the trust and distribute the property in the trust (page 115, Article XI).

The law of most states precludes a trust from going on forever. The statute which does this is called the *Rule Against Perpetuities*. This is perhaps the least understood concept in the law. However, if the trust violates that law, the entire trust can be void. The trust should contain a *savings clause*. This is a provision which states that the trust will terminate automatically at the end of the perpetuities period (page 123, Article XXIV).

Here again, when you execute a living trust, you should observe the proper formalities. A trust should be executed with all of the formalities of a deed. The signature or signatures of the settlor or the settlors should be witnessed, and the settlors should acknowledge before a notary public that they intended to settle the trust. You do not need to witness the signatures of trustees or successor trustees. These persons are only signing a contract, and a contract does not need to be witnessed unless there is a specific statute which requires witnesses.

After you have executed your trust documents, you transfer the property which is registered in your name into the trust. Alfred A. Smith and Betty B. Smith, for example, would put property into their joint living trust, registering it in the name of "Alfred A. Smith and

Betty B. Smith, Trustees of the Alfred and Betty Smith Living Trust, dated December 7, 1991." In effect, you are probating your own will while you are alive. You put land into your trust by means of a quit-claim deed from yourselves to yourselves as trustees of your living trust. (See letter on page 169.)

The terms which lawyers have used to describe the person who establishes a trust have varied through the years. Most estate-planning attorneys call such a person a settlor, for that person settles a trust. However, you can settle a trust by a *declaration* that you are holding certain property as trustee for the benefit of yourself or someone else. In such a case, you are the *declarant*. You can also *grant* property to someone with strings of trusteeship attached. In that case, you would be the *grantor*. To round things off, if you are making a gift by way of a trust, you can call yourself the *donor* of the trust.

The *Internal Revenue Code* (IRC), with its typical disdain for simplicity, refers to a self-directed living trust as a *grantor trust*. Prior to January 1, 1981, all trusts were tax-paying entities, and the trustee of any trust was required to obtain an *employer identification number* for the trust and to report any income with respect to the trust property on Form 1041. However, since that date, the trustee of a grantor trust neither applies for an employee identification number nor reports trust income on Form 1041. Instead, the beneficiaries report the income on their Form 1040.

The reason for this is so simple that it is amazing that the Internal Revenue Service (IRS) ever understood it. There is no conceivable way that a self-directed living trust would ever pay any tax, all of the income being effectively distributed to the settlor each year. For many years, people who had self-directed living trusts submitted a Form 1041 which always showed that the trust owed no income tax. Hard to believe?

There is a letter beginning on page 165 which shows exactly what the tax regulation is and how it applies.

You will find an example of a living trust for a couple with a small estate beginning on page 109. We have explained the purpose of the various articles in the trust on pages 1 through 3 of the letter explaining the estate-planning documents beginning at page 103.

You should find the trust agreement relatively easy to read. The legal community is attempting to get lawyers to write in "plain English." It is not easy for an older attorney to stop referring to his "aforementioned said wife, hereinafter referred to as Mary." Young attorneys sometimes use "legalese" to make them sound more like a lawyer. The result is all too often a document which reads as though it were written by a plumber.

If you do not understand something in a document which a lawyer gives you to review, ask about it. Never sign something you do not understand. On the other hand, make every effort to understand the document. A lawyer cannot take the time to rewrite everything for you unless you are willing to pay a very large fee. Your lawyer can explain your documents to you in such a manner that you can understand them if you want to.

CHAPTER 7

Special Provisions for Young Children

IF YOU HAVE minor children, you may know someone whom you would want to have appointed as *guardian* or *guardians* of these children in the event that you and your spouse, if you have one, were both deceased. Although you can leave your property to anyone you wish, you cannot leave your children to someone. The probate court has complete discretion as to who will be appointed as guardian or guardians. The court will consider the welfare of the children above everything else.

If you want to have a specific guardian or guardians appointed for your children, you can put a provision in your will directing the personal representative of the estate to seek to have a specific person or persons named in your will, or the person or persons most recently named in a letter held by the successor trustee, appointed as the guardian or guardians of your children. In this letter, you give your reasons for this selection. The letter remains sealed until your death, and avoids offending any persons whom you have not selected. When

35

your youngest child is eighteen years of age, you can destroy the letter.

In the event of your death while one or more of your children are under the age of eighteen years, the successor trustee delivers the letter to the personal representative, who petitions the probate court for the appointment. The court will give a great deal of attention to such a request, because you are in a better position than anyone to know what is good for your children.

The probate court will not normally put the management of money for minors in the hands of the guardians for the minors. To do so would create a conflict of interest. A person managing property has discretion to pay money to the guardians for the needs of the children. The court does not want people to have discretion to pay themselves money belonging to children.

Unless you have a trust, either living or created by your will, all of the property which you leave to a minor will be delivered on the minor's eighteenth birthday. It takes very little imagination to see how property which could give a child a wonderful start in life could spell the child's doom.

In the case of children or grandchildren where the parent has died and the grandchildren are the beneficiaries of the deceased parent's share of a trust, we accumulate the earnings until the child reaches eighteen years of age. During this period, we permit the trustee to invade the trust for medical expenses, education and support, taking into consideration any other sources of support for the child of which the trustee is aware, such as social security payments to the guardians for the benefit of the child.

After age eighteen, the trustee will pay the income from the trust property but will retain the principal. If the trustee accumulates earnings after the child is eighteen years old, the child will have to amend all of the tax returns from age eighteen to the time of distribution under the *throwback rules* of the Internal Revenue Code.

We generally have the distribution of the principal in two or three installments, depending on the size of the trust. For example, the trustee can pay one-third of the money at age twenty-five and the remainder at age thirty, or the trustee can pay one-fourth at age twenty-five, one-third of the balance at age thirty, and the remainder at age thirty-five.

Whenever the beneficiaries of a trust are children, incompetent persons, or very old people, you should consider having a corporate trustee manage the trust property and carry out the trust provisions. A corporate trustee is limited to *investment grade securities* when it is managing property for beneficiaries who are not the settlors of the trust. Their idea of a risky investment is something like Detroit Edison common stock. They won't lose the money in the trust. Indeed, they'll make you rich, but not quickly.

Corporate trustees are skilled at making discretionary decisions. For example, a young beneficiary wants to get braces on her teeth. The trustee would ask, "If mother and father were here and had set this money aside for this girl, would they pay for the braces?" The answer is obvious. When an aunt or uncle is to make discretionary decisions, the ground is fertile for the growth of animosity within the family. Corporate trustees consult with senior family members and then take full responsibility for the decision. The system works very well.

CHAPTER 8

Authority to Give or Withhold Medical Treatment

NANCY CRUZAN WAS in a coma with little hope that she would ever again regain consciousness. She did not require any mechanical means of life support, but she was receiving all of her nourishment through a tube. Her family sought to terminate the procedure which was providing her nutrition in order to permit her to "die with dignity."

Missouri law requires medical people to use their best efforts to preserve human life. Effectively, Missouri law does not permit anyone other than the patient to order the discontinuation of life-support systems, including nutritional support. Since Nancy was not conscious, she could not make that decision for herself. The Missouri court refused to issue the order, which her family sought. The United States Supreme Court upheld the decision of the Missouri court, stating that the state's interest in preserving life must prevail over the family's interest in terminating the treatment.

However, the Supreme Court went on to state that if the Missouri Court had known, by *clear and convincing evidence*, what Nancy would have wanted, her wishes would be entitled to constitutional protection. This had a dramatic effect on the legal consequences of a *Declaration to Physicians* or *living will* throughout the United States.

It has been well established in our courts that an adult who is competent to manage his or her affairs has the right to refuse any medical treatment, including withholding or withdrawing life-support systems and the application of nutrition and hydration systems. This right is guaranteed as part of our "Right of Privacy" under the First Amendment to the Constitution of the United States of America.

Only a competent person can make that decision for himself or herself. The importance of the Cruzan case is that the Supreme Court has now stated that a person can preserve this constitutional right by providing others with "clear and convincing evidence" of the desire that life-support systems not be used under certain circumstances. The living will provides the mechanism to do this. The only questions that remain concern the language which the living will must contain to be effective and what formalities must be used in its execution.

Attorneys who practice in this area of the law seem to agree that if you wish to demonstrate your desires in a living will by "clear and convincing evidence," you must state specifically what your desires are. For example, your living will must state that you "direct that life-sustaining procedures be withheld or withdrawn" and that you "be permitted to die naturally, with only the administration of medical procedures deemed necessary to alleviate pain," or that you "further direct that nutrition and hydration be withheld or withdrawn when the application of such procedures would serve only to prolong artificially the process of dying." Many states have enacted legislation stating this requirement.

We all hope that we will never find ourselves or any member of our family in Nancy's situation. The problem we face is that it could happen to any of us, and it could happen in any state in the country. We do not know what the laws of that state may be.

In order to preclude the question of proper execution from arising in another state, it is wise to execute any legal document in accordance with the most rigid requirements of formality for that type of document. With this in mind, if you decide to execute a living will, do it with the same formalities as you would use for a Last Will and Testament. The document should also include a *Proof of Declaration* which is executed with the same formalities as we use with a Proof of Will.

The living will takes care of the situation wherever you are going to die no matter what the doctors do, and you are unable to give directions. However, if you need medical attention and are unable to give permission, you need a different type of document. This document is known as a *Power of Attorney for Medical Care*. The document recites that if you are unable to give instructions, the person designated in the document can make medical decisions for you. The designated person could be your spouse with an adult child as an alternative for the time when your spouse is either deceased or incompetent to make the decision. You can use a similar power of attorney to give parental powers to persons such as grandparents when the grandchildren are staying with their grandparents for a prolonged period of time, such as a vacation.

You will find a sample of the living will which is suitable for a man or for an older woman beginning on page 143. There is a living will suitable for a young woman beginning on page 145. Both of these documents contain a Proof of Declaration. The difference between them is that the living will for a young woman contains paragraph three, which deals with pregnancy.

There are four powers of attorney for medical care on pages 147, 149, 151, and 154. All of these powers are contingent upon the disability of the person granting the power. For instance, the husband and the wife have each granted a medical power to each other. However, in the normal course of events, one of them will predecease the other. If one of them were to become incompetent and then the other were to die, it would be too late to avoid a probate proceeding to appoint a guardian. That is the reason why each of them has granted a medical power to their son which becomes effective when the person granting the power becomes incompetent and the other spouse is either deceased or also incompetent.

CHAPTER 9

The Power of Attorney

A MAN WAS given the opportunity to elect whether he wanted to receive a lump-sum payment from his pension plan or receive an annuity which would pay him a certain amount each month for life. He had to make the election before the end of the year or the plan would automatically become an annuity. He suffered a stroke in the middle of November and was alive and conscious, but incompetent to conduct business. There was little doubt that he would not be able to elect the lump-sum payment. If the pension became an annuity, his wife would receive nothing from his pension after his death.

The man's wife engaged an attorney to have her appointed as his guardian for all purposes. This would give her the power to elect to withdraw the money from the pension fund. The attorney submitted the petition to the probate court, gathered affidavits from the doctors, and attended the hearing at which the wife was appointed guardian. The attorney fees were $1,100. The probate court appointed another attorney as *guardian ad litem* for the incompetent husband. A guardian ad litem is a guardian only for this matter who is appointed to ensure that the wife was not working a number on her husband. This attorney visited the husband in the hospital and appeared at the hearing. This attorney's fee was $600. The court also appointed a committee of three persons to review the wife's *plan of guardianship*, which the wife was to submit at a later date. The court fee for this committee was $400. The wife made the election, and the husband died just after the first of the year.

The guardianship proceedings were not yet finished. The wife still had to submit a plan of guardianship to be approved by the committee and submit an accounting for any money she had received. Her husband left no probate estate because of joint ownership and payable-on-death provisions. His wife received about $1,700 in social security checks after being appointed guardian and before her husband's death.

The husband should have executed a *durable power of attorney* during the time when he was competent. A power of attorney is a document which appoints someone to be your *attorney-in-fact*. With such a document, you can give someone the power to do anything which the law empowers you to do. Any power of attorney terminates with the death of the person granting it because the person granting it is not legally empowered to do anything when he is no longer living.

A power of attorney normally terminates when the person granting it is no longer competent. An incompetent person does not have the power to make business decisions, and the power only grants to another the power to do the things which you can do yourself. Most states have enacted statutes which permit a power of attorney to continue in effect even after the person who granted the power becomes incompetent. A power of attorney which continues to operate in this manner is said to be *durable*. You can even grant a power of attorney which does not become effective until and unless you become incompetent to handle your own affairs. This is known as a *contingent durable power of attorney*.

You would normally grant a *general power of attorney* to your spouse. This empowers your spouse to do all things necessary to carry out the purposes of the family. There may be times when you would want to grant a *limited power of attorney* to someone else. This is a power of attorney to do some specific thing, such as negotiate a car title or close a land deal.

In estate planning, the settlor of a trust often grants a *contingent limited durable power of attorney* to the successor trustee. The trust contains a provision by which the successor trustee becomes the trustee if a settlor who is also the trustee becomes incompetent. We never want a lapse of management for property. There should always be someone who can pay taxes, utilities, and so forth. However, the successor trustee can only manage property which is in the trust. The contingent power of attorney grants the successor trustee the limited power to transfer property into the trust when the settlor has neglected to do so.

The living will, the contingent power of attorney, and the contingent medical power of attorney are all things which we hope you will never need. However, if you do need any of these documents and don't have them, keep your checkbook handy. You will have to make an appearance in front of that person sitting on the elevated bench wearing the black robe. You will note that every estate-planning document which we create points toward your not having to spend additional money on lawyers and judges.

There are four sample powers of attorney in the appendix on pages 159, 161, and 163. For example, both husband and wife have granted a general power of attorney to each other which becomes effective in the event of incompetence. Each of them has also granted a limited power of attorney to the successor trustee of their living trust. The logic of having four powers is the same as the logic of having four medical powers of attorney. In the normal course of events, one spouse will predecease the other. If one of them were to become incompetent and then the other were to die, it would be too late to avoid a probate proceeding to appoint a guardian. The successor trustee would begin to manage the assets in the trust, but it could do nothing about assets which the settlors had forgotten to put into the trust. The contingent power granted to the successor is limited to transferring assets into the living trust, which the settlors have created. This situation does not arise often, but when it does, this tool can be very valuable.

CHAPTER 10

The Federal Gift and Estate Tax

THE FEDERAL GIFT and Estate Tax is imposed upon persons making gifts. The person who receives a gift is not taxed by the federal government. Every gift which you make during your lifetime and upon your death is taxed under the provisions of the Federal Gift and Estate Tax portion of the IRC, unless the gift qualifies for the $10,000 *annual exclusion*, is a *charitable gift*, or is offset by the *unlimited marital deduction*.

In other words, you can make as many gifts of $10,000 per individual to anyone without paying any tax on the gift, if the gift qualifies for the annual exclusion. Furthermore, you can make any number of gifts of any size to a charity without paying any tax on the gift provided the gift qualifies as a charitable donation. Finally, you can give your spouse any amount you wish without paying any tax on the gift if the property qualifies for the unlimited marital deduction. The gift and estate tax has nothing to do with the tax which is imposed under the Income Tax sections of the IRC. The two systems are independent but parallel.

The gift and estate tax is a graduated tax which begins with the first dollar of gifts which you make. IRC grants each one of us a *unified credit* of $192,600 which we can use to offset any gift or estate tax obligations which we incur. It just so happens that the tax on $600,000 is $192,600 and we use our entire unified credit when we make a gift or gifts of $600,000 or more.

This is why we can give gifts totalling $600,000 during our lifetime and at death without incurring any tax. However, you see that the mechanism is in place for the United States Congress to raise your taxes.

Many states impose an inheritance tax upon estates. This tax is imposed upon the person who receives the gift, rather than upon the giver. In 1982, the federal government made gifts between spouses exempt from taxation, and most states followed by doing the same thing. Thus, most inheritance taxes are only imposed upon gifts to persons other than spouses. In most states, if a person owns property jointly with another for a period of years (with right of survivorship) and becomes the sole owner as a result of the other person's death, there is no inheritance tax. State inheritance taxes do not even begin to approach the burden of the Federal Estate Tax.

The Federal Gift and Estate Tax and the Federal Income Tax run parallel to each other. There is a principle which permeates the IRC that everything which anyone receives, other than the return of his or her own money, shall be taxed. Here is how that works. If I were to make an *inter vivos*, or lifetime, gift to you of $1,000 worth of General Motors stock for which I had paid $100, your basis in the stock would be the same as mine—$100. If you were to sell the stock for $1,000, you would pay income tax on $900, the difference between your basis in the stock and the amount you received. However, if I were to leave you the same $1,000 worth of stock in my will, you would take the stock with a basis of the fair market value of the stock as of the date of my death.

Anything you receive by inheritance receives this *stepped-up basis*. The reason for this is that I paid Federal Estate Tax on the gift to you. I may have paid money to the federal government, or I may have used part of my unified credit to pay the tax. The logic is not complete, for the inter vivos gift is also taxable under the IRC.

The IRC lets us vary the *valuation date*, or the date on which the fair-market value of the assets in someone's estate is determined. The estate can make an election as to whether the assets should be valued at the date of the decedent's death or six months later. The lesson here is simple: when property has *appreciated* in value, we give it away at death so that it will receive the stepped-up basis.

Community-property states provide a special opportunity to receive a stepped-up basis. Assume that a husband and wife own their home as community property in a community-property state, and they paid $50,000 for the home which is now worth $250,000. As community property, each owns half of the home. However, if the husband dies holding the home jointly with his wife, the wife receives a stepped-up basis on the entire parcel.

The interesting thing about this situation is that if a couple acquired community property in Texas and then moved to Florida, the property retains its community-property character. The community-property concept has not been lost on estate-planning attorneys. They draft a joint trust to deal with the community property so that appreciated community property receives a stepped-up basis upon the first death.

It should not surprise you to know that even people with large estates often die without doing any estate tax planning. When this occurs, all is not lost, but part of it is. For example, when one spouse of a couple with a large estate dies, the surviving spouse may be able to *disclaim* part of the property coming from the deceased spouse. The effect of this *disclaimer* is to have the disclaimed property go to the children. The gift to the children would be taxable and could use the deceased spouse's unified credit. The potential tax savings is again about $240,000 if the total estate is over $1,200,000. Unfortunately, the surviving spouse will not have the income from the disclaimed property. You will see in the following chapter how this couple could have placed their property into living trusts under which the surviving spouse would receive this income.

Whenever someone with exposure to the Federal Estate Tax dies without any tax planning, always seek the advice of good tax lawyers and CPAs. Even when there is no requirement for probate of the estate, there may be ways for the trustee to sell or transfer property with substantial tax savings through *post mortem*, or after-death, tax planning.

There are basically six ways in which we can reduce the tax which will be imposed upon the part of a person's estate which is over $600,000. Every tax-avoidance scheme has some disadvantage or another. You gain tax relief and you lose something. This chapter describes briefly the six types of schemes which lawyers have devised to reduce your exposure to this tax.

1. By *using living trusts* an estate-planning attorney can arrange the affairs of a married couple in such a manner that the couple will

pay no estate tax upon the death of the first of them and will pay no estate tax on the first $1,200,000 of their estate. Tax savings—about $240,000. However, if the estate of an individual without a spouse is over $600,000, or the estate of a married couple is over $1,200,000, the estate will be exposed to the gift and estate tax to the extent it exceeds these amounts.

In an estate which is over $600,000, each spouse creates his or her own living trust. Depending on how they handle their family affairs, each can be the trustee of his or her own trust, they can both be trustees of both trusts, or one of them can be trustee of both trusts. We then put one-half of the family property into each trust.

Each trust states that when one spouse dies, we put up to $600,000 into a *tax shelter trust (Trust B)* and put the rest of the property from the deceased spouse's trust into the surviving spouse's trust. The surviving spouse gets all of the income from Trust B during lifetime, and the property in Trust B goes to the children when the surviving spouse dies. There is no tax on the ultimate gift from the deceased spouse to the children, for it is an amount of $600,000 or less. There is no tax on the gift from the deceased spouse to the surviving spouse, because the gift qualifies for the unlimited marital deduction. When the surviving spouse dies, the property in that trust goes to the children. Any amount over $600,000 will be subject to the Federal Estate Tax, but a total amount of $1,200,000 passed to the children, tax free.

2. We can *reduce the size of an estate* by making annual gifts to our children, grandchildren, and our children's spouses in the amount of $10,000 or less. The disadvantage of this method is that we are intentionally making ourselves poorer, and we may need the money at some time in the future. However, for someone with an estate which will be taxed at the rate of 50%, the government pays one-half of any gift.

If these gifts are for the benefit of minors, you may want to make the gift to a *Child's Savings Trust* where the child does not receive a check at the age of eighteen years, for reasons of management. For large estates, this type of trust not only *reduces the tax imposed upon the estate*, but it *avoids the tax on the gift* and *avoids the generation-skipping tax on gifts made to grandchildren* who are present beneficiaries.

3. We can *reduce the size of an estate tax* and *substitute payments to beneficiaries in the amount of the estate tax* through the use of

47

life insurance. This offers a different type of solution to two problems presented by the tax imposed upon very large estates. These are as follows:

a. *Availability of Cash to Pay Tax.* If the estate does not have sufficient cash to pay the tax, the proceeds from the life insurance can provide this cash at the time it will be needed. If necessary, the beneficiaries of the life insurance can lend money to the estate so that the estate will not find it necessary to sell assets at a time when they will not bring a good price.

For example, a widower died leaving an estate which was subject to several hundred thousand dollars of federal tax. There was very little cash in the estate. It consisted primarily of a $450,000 home and a very valuable partnership interest. The partnership had an arrangement under which the surviving partners would purchase a deceased partner's interest over a period of ten years. The market for large homes was depressed at the time. The widower's children lent the estate cash from the proceeds from an insurance policy on the life of the deceased, and the estate was not forced to sell the home in a depressed market.

b. *Replacement of the Tax Payment.* If the proceeds from an insurance policy on the life of a deceased, payable to the children of the deceased, are as large as the tax which will be imposed upon the estate, the children of the deceased will receive the same net amount as they would if the tax were not imposed. For example, if the federal tax imposed on an estate is $500,000, the amount which the children of the deceased will receive from the estate will be reduced by $500,000. However, if the children were to receive the proceeds from a $500,000 life-insurance policy, they would be in the same position as they would be if there were no life-insurance policy and there were no federal tax.

Remember, for someone with an estate which will be taxed at the rate of 50% under the Federal Gift and Estate Tax, the government effectively pays one-half of any life-insurance premium. The amount of the premium will not be included in the estate if the gift is made in such a manner that the payment itself is not a gift. The benefits of life insurance as an estate-planning tool are enhanced by the interesting treatment of the proceeds from life insurance under both the income tax sections and the gift and estate tax sections of the IRC.

a. *The Insurance Policy Belongs to the Beneficiaries.* If the insured person or persons retains *no incidents of ownership* in a policy of life insurance upon his or her life, neither the value of the policy nor the proceeds from the policy will be included in his or her estate for estate tax purposes. This is logical. It is very important that the insured person does not retain such powers as the right to borrow against the policy or change the beneficiaries. As a rule of thumb, if the insured has no more rights than he or she would have had if someone else had purchased the policy, the incidents of ownership rule will be satisfied and the proceeds from the life-insurance policy will not be included in the insured's estate for estate tax purposes.

b. *No Tax to the Recipient of the Death Benefit*. The proceeds from life insurance are not taxed to the recipient as income. This is somewhat more difficult to justify. The proceeds from the life insurance policy will often be more than the premiums paid on the policy. There would appear to be a gain on the entire transaction which could be subject to income tax. There are reasons for not imposing income tax upon these proceeds, but we won't go into them here.

4. We can *reduce the size of the taxable estate* by creating an *Irrevocable Charitable Remainder Trust*. This trust provides that the person or persons who create the trust receive the income from the property in the trust during lifetime, and directs the trustee to convey the assets in the trust to some charity or charities upon death.

The person who gives the property to the trust receives a *charitable deduction* in the amount of the *present value of the future gift* for income tax purposes, and the value of the property is effectively not included in his or her estate for estate tax.

This can be a valuable technique for increasing the yield on investments which have appreciated in value and have a low yield on their present fair-market value. The trustee sells the appreciated property and reinvests it in property with a higher yield. Since the trust is a charity and not taxed upon its gain, the trust pays no tax on that gain.

The person who established the trust can conceivably receive more by giving the property to a charity than by keeping the property. The disadvantage of this method is that the children of the person or persons who established the trust will not receive the property.

5. We can *reduce the value of the gifts which are taxed* by creating an *Irrevocable Grantor Retained Income Trust, Grantor Retained Unitrust*, or a *Grantor Retained Annuity Trust*. These are trusts in which the person or couple who sets up the trust receives the income from or the use of the property which they

49

put into the trust for a period, but makes a present gift of the future use of the property. This still creates a taxable gift, but the *value* of the gift is reduced. The tax is imposed only upon the *present value of the future interest.*

6. We can *freeze the value of the estate* by preventing the assets in the estate from increasing in value. For example, if someone owns a parcel of commercial property which is rather certain to increase in value, that person can have the parcel appraised and then sell it to his or her children at its fair-market value under the terms of an installment contract. The children make the payments due under the contract from the income which they receive from the property and do not have to recognize the gain on the future appreciation in value until they sell it. This does not decrease the size of the estate, and the parent must pay income tax on the gain which results from the sale.

Under certain circumstances the technique can be of great value. We can do something similar to this with the family business if the parents are ready to turn it over to their children. The attorney must structure this sort of arrangement very carefully, or the tax results can be very different from what we want.

Whenever you are using a tax-avoidance scheme of any sort, you should review the documents which implement the scheme whenever there is a significant change in the tax law. Estate-planning attorneys try to inform their clients of changes which require action. However, if the attorney does a great deal of estate planning it is likely that he will not notice that a certain estate needs attention.

CHAPTER 11

The Split Estate

WHENEVER YOU ARE going to do something for the purpose of avoiding tax, you should make your way of doing it very similar to the method which every other kid in town is using. There is a classic way to organize the large estate of a married couple. We "split" the estate using two trusts.

When a married couple treats all of the children of each spouse as being children of the marriage, we create reciprocal trusts in which each spouse leaves everything to the other and then divides the property among all the children of both spouses equally upon the death of the second spouse. Each spouse is the settlor of his or her living trust. Each trust directs the trustee to put as much property into the tax shelter trust (Trust B) as the settlor can give without incurring any estate tax if the settlor is survived by his or her spouse. The trust directs the trustee to put all of the property into Trust B if the settlor is not survived by his or her spouse.

If the settlor has not made any taxable gifts during lifetime, this provision will put $600,000 into Trust B. The trustee will put the remainder of the property from the deceased settlor's trust into the

51

living trust of the surviving spouse. Trust B is for the benefit of the settlor's children and is taxable. However, there will be no tax on the gift, because the settlor can use the unified credit to pay the tax. The gift to the surviving spouse's trust is not taxable, for it will qualify for the unlimited marital deduction.

There will be no estate tax owing when only one of the spouses dies. When the second spouse dies, the estate will be liable for any amount of tax exceeding the second spouse's unified credit.

Trust B contains the following four provisions:

1. The surviving spouse shall receive all of the income from the property which is in Trust B.
2. The trustee shall have discretion to pay for necessary education, comfortable maintenance, and medical care for the surviving spouse, considering other sources of income which the surviving spouse may have.
3. The surviving spouse shall have an unrestricted, noncumulative right to withdraw the greater of 5% or $5,000 from the principal of the trust each year.
4. Upon the death of the surviving spouse, or upon the death of the settlor if he or she survived his or her spouse, the trustee shall distribute the property as directed in the trust agreement.

When our married couple first set up their trusts, they should enter into a *Property Ownership Agreement*. This agreement looks a great deal like a divorce settlement agreement, but neither should plan to hide behind the agreement in the event of divorce. It is designed to be binding upon the IRS with respect to the division of property. It recites that the couple has made gifts to each other in order to divide the property to accomplish a proper tax-avoidance purpose.

The property agreement lists the property which belongs to the husband and the property which belongs to the wife. Each of them then executes either a *Conveyance to Trustee* or a *Declaration of Trust* for the property which the agreement says they own. If both of them are trustees of both trusts, each of them executes a conveyance to both of them as trustees. If each of them is the trustee of their own trusts, each of them executes a declaration that they hold the property as trustee. In other words, you make a conveyance to trustee(s) to someone else or yourself and someone else, and you do a declaration of trust if you are your own sole trustee.

We handle the ultimate distribution of property in a split estate in the same manner as the ultimate distribution of any property. That is to say, we make provision for management of property for young people and deal with other management problems in a similar manner. However, if the ultimate distribution is to grandchildren with living parents, a total of gifts in excess of $1,000,000 will be subject to the *generation skipping tax*. You pay tax on the gift to both your children and your grandchildren.

CHAPTER 12

Yours, Mine, and Ours—The Second Marriage

THE LAW HAS always favored marriage. As a matter of public policy, the common law and the statutes which have been enacted have always rewarded those who marry and remain married until the death of their spouse.

Beginning in ancient times, the law protected the surviving spouse under concepts called *dower* and *curtesy*. The word "curtesy" is not misspelled in this context. A widow's dower rights gave her a *life estate* in one-third of all real property which her husband owned during the marriage. Curtesy was a somewhat similar doctrine. A surviving husband was awarded a life estate in all the lands which his wife owned during the marriage, by "curtesy" of the law of England. The concept of dower continued in almost every state in America, but the concept of curtesy did not.

The reasons why dower continued to be the law in America are entangled in an unarticulated public policy which has permeated the probate courts. The courts have always seemed to be intent on "taking care of the widows and orphans." Any deed which a married man signed would convey the land subject to his wife's dower rights, unless she joined in the conveyance. Remember, in ancient times, only the land had value. This not only prevented a married man from selling the family farm in between poker hands, but it also prevented a married man from leaving everything to his sweetheart to the exclusion of his loving and faithful wife.

Neither dower nor curtesy gave a surviving spouse any rights in a deceased spouse's personal property. In other words, a married man could still give his stocks, bonds, and bank accounts to anyone he wished. In many states, dower and curtesy have been abolished in favor of statutes which give the surviving spouse the election of taking under the terms of the deceased spouse's will or taking a percentage of the deceased spouse's probate estate.

This did not solve the problem completely. When dower existed, a husband could not convey land without the land being subject to his wife's dower, unless she was willing to join in the conveyance. When dower was replaced by an elective share, either spouse could convey real or personal property which he or she held in his or her own name without the necessity of any agreement between the spouses.

The Wisconsin legislature has attempted to address these problems by adopting the Wisconsin Marital Property Act (which is almost identical to the Uniform Marital Property Act proposed by the National Conference of Commissioners of Uniform State Laws). This gives Wisconsin something rather similar to community property.

Under the Wisconsin act, each marital partner retains his or her rights to property which he or she brought into the marriage as *separate property*. Any property acquired during the marriage is *marital property*. The two of them share equally in any income or profits earned during the marriage, including any income from their separate property.

Presently, in most states, either spouse can defeat the other spouse's right to an elective share of his or her probate estate by giving property away during lifetime. In certain cases, this can be unfair. The concept of a *fraud against the marriage* has developed in opposition to a spouse's right to do this. Florida is a leader in the development of this concept. Under Florida law, a spouse can give anything during his or her lifetime, provided it is his or her separate property and the gift is a complete divestment of his or her interest in the property.

On April 12, 1990, the 5th District Court of Appeals in Florida decided a case in which a wife claimed that her deceased husband had committed a fraud upon the marriage. Carol E. Donahue, Esquire, of Winter Park, Florida, argued the case for the appellant, Joan Traub. The Traubs were in the process of a divorce when the deceased husband gave his children from a prior marriage almost all of his wealth prior to his death. The court held as follows:

> . . . The doctrine of fraud on marital rights represents an effort to balance the social and practical undesirability of restricting the free alienation of personal property against the desire to protect the legal share of a spouse. It has always been recognized that a husband, in the absence of statutory regulation like that in the case of dower, has an unqualified right to give away his personal property during his lifetime, even though the effect is to deprive the wife of her statutory share. But *if the gift is not absolute and unconditional* and *the donor retains dominion and control over the property during his lifetime,* the courts have held that the gift is colorable and may be set aside. . . . 559 So.2d 443 (Fla. App. 5 Dist. 1990), p. 446 (emphasis added)

Mrs. Traub lost her appeal because the gifts which her deceased husband had made were complete, and Mrs. Traub could not elect to claim her elective share of this property upon Mr. Traub's death. Mrs. Traub could not make this property part of Mr. Traub's probate estate.

The Florida court appears to have said that it would have set the conveyances aside if Mr. Traub had merely placed the assets in a revocable living trust which contained the standard terms permitting him to name the trustee, take property out of the trust whenever he wanted, and permitting him to change the distribution of trust assets upon his death. Under these conditions, the transfer would not be "absolute and unconditional."

If the court had set aside the conveyances which Mr. Traub made to his living trust, these assets would be in Mr. Traub's probate estate and his widow, Joan Traub, would have been able to elect to take 30% of his estate under Florida law in lieu of whatever he decided to leave to her under the terms of his living trust or his will.

Both the Florida concept of a fraud upon the marriage and marital property acts such as the one in Wisconsin can cause as many problems as they solve in a situation in which one or both marital partners have already been married to someone else. For example, one or both partners who enter into a marriage may now be single as the result of divorce or the death of the prior spouse. In such cases, they may have accumulated property and may have children from the prior marriage to whom they wish to leave their separate property upon their death.

Even if both partners to a second marriage agree as to what should be the disposition of their property in the event of a divorce or upon death, their plans can be frustrated by the very laws which were put in place to prevent injustice. For example, if they put everything into joint ownership it becomes "winner take all," and the children of the first to die are left out in the cold. If each of them makes a will, the surviving spouse can elect against the will and distort the distribution to the detriment of the deceased spouse's children.

Remember, if one spouse becomes incompetent before the other dies, one of the surviving incompetent spouse's children will be in a position to make the election against the terms of the deceased spouse's will as legal guardian of the incompetent spouse. This election could include a petition to the probate court to set aside the deceased spouse's conveyances to a living trust.

The solution to all of these problems is very simple. If the marital partners can agree upon what they want, an attorney can prepare documents which will carry out their scheme of distribution no matter which one may die first—even if one or both of them become incompetent. Once they have committed their agreement to writing, each should seek the advice of his or her own attorney. After they have signed the agreement, they can organize their affairs in such a manner that: (1) they avoid taxes to the maximum extent possible; (2) they avoid the necessity for any probate of either estate; and (3) their plans will be carried out no matter who dies first.

Once the couple has agreed what should happen after the death of one of them or upon the common death of both, they enter into a property ownership agreement. This agreement is somewhat different from the agreement which a couple with a long marriage and the desire to save their estates from the tax collector would sign.

The agreement recites that this is the second marriage, that each spouse has property which he or she brought into the marriage, and which each spouse wants to give his or her children at some time in the future. The agreement further recites that the couple has joint property which the survivor would use and which would be distributed in a specific manner after both spouses are deceased. The articles in the agreement specify the property which belongs to each spouse and the property which they own as joint property. Finally, the agreement specifies that they have reached agreement on a plan of ultimate distribution of all property through trusts.

The IRC makes provision for a second marriage trust. This has been referred to as "The Senators' Trust," because senators have had a tendency to divorce their wives of many years and marry their secretaries. They want to utilize the secretary's unified credit, and they want to take care of her during her lifetime, but they don't want any of their money to go to "that kid of hers."

The IRC authorizes the *Qualified Terminal Interest Property Trust* (QTIP). Most split estate trust agreements refer to this as Trust C. Normally, *terminal interest property* does not qualify for the unlimited marital deduction and would be taxed as part of the deceased's estate.

Terminal interest property is property in which the ownership of the person to whom it is given terminates with reference to the death of the person who made the gift. However, under the IRC, one spouse can put property into the QTIP trust, give the other spouse the use of the property during lifetime, have the property distributed to the children of the deceased spouse upon the death of the surviving spouse, and have the value of the property taxed as part of the surviving spouse's estate rather than the deceased spouse's estate. Normally, Trust C contains a provision stating that the trustee will pay any additional estate tax which is imposed on the surviving spouse's estate as a result of the inclusion of this property.

Trust C contains the following four provisions:

1. The surviving spouse shall receive all of the income from the property which is in Trust C.
2. The Trustee has discretion to pay such sums from the principal of Trust C as may be necessary for the medical care, education, support, and maintenance in reasonable comfort of the surviving spouse.
3. The surviving spouse may require the Trustee either to make any nonproductive property of the trust productive or to convert any nonproductive property to productive property within a reasonable time.
4. Upon the death of the surviving spouse, the trustee shall distribute the property as directed in the trust agreement.

Depending on the circumstances, such as the amount of separate property which the surviving spouse may own, Trust C may contain a fifth provision directing the trustee to pay any additional estate tax, which may be imposed upon the surviving spouse's estate as a result of the property in Trust C being included in that estate for estate tax purposes.

Again we see that the family of the surviving spouse in a second marriage could do very well in the event that the marriage partners do not agree upon what should be done ultimately and take such actions as are necessary to see that their wishes are carried out. Remember, the law favors marriage, and the courts will enforce your agreement if they can. Commit your agreement to writing and provide the mechanism to carry it out.

We have used examples from the laws in Florida and Wisconsin. The law varies a great deal from state to state. Be certain that you check with an attorney as to what the law is in the state where you reside.

CHAPTER 13

The Children's Savings Trust

THERE ARE TWO common reasons why people set aside money for children:

First, parents or grandparents may wish to ensure that money is available for the child's advanced education.

Second, persons with very large estates may wish to avoid some of the federal estate tax which will be imposed upon their estates at death *by reducing the size of their estates*. One of the ways of doing this is by making annual gifts of $10,000 or less to a child or grandchild. If they do so properly, these gifts will fall under the annual exclusion to the Federal Gift and Estate Tax. If a person whose estate will be taxed at a marginal rate of 50% at death makes a tax exempt gift of $10,000, the estate will be reduced by $10,000, and the federal estate tax imposed upon the estate will be $5,000 less. In effect, the government is paying one-half of the $10,000 gift.

If a series of gifts to a child amount to thousands of dollars, we would not want the child to receive the entire amount on his or her eighteenth birthday. The proper way to distribute the money is through the mechanism of a Child's Savings Trust. The persons who establish such a trust may also be the trustees of the trust.

The trustee has discretion to pay unusual expenses for the child from the outset. These might include medical, dental, and educational expenses. For example, if the child takes up playing the violin and gets a chance to go to the National Music Camp at Interlochen, the trustee could pay the tuition and housing. Although the child will receive a great deal of money at some future date, he or she will never be fifteen again with such an opportunity.

Once the child reaches the age of eighteen years, the trustee should pay the child all of the income from the trust assets. Again, if the trustee accumulates the income, the beneficiary will have to amend all of his or her income tax returns for the years in which the trustee accumulated the income under the throwback rules of the IRC.

It is entirely possible that the income from the trust assets will be insufficient to meet the beneficiary's educational needs. For this reason, the trustee should have discretion to continue to invade the principal for education and maintenance. For example, if the beneficiary is admitted to Harvard Medical School, it would take a very large trust, indeed, to produce enough income to pay the tuition and housing. Even if the prime purpose of the trust was to reduce the size of a very large estate, there is almost invariably a strong secondary purpose of benefit to the beneficiary.

In every trust, other than a charitable trust, there is an event which triggers the final distribution of the trust assets. In a child's savings trust, that event is usually the age of the beneficiary. For example, we might distribute one-third of the trust principal to the beneficiary when the beneficiary attains the age of twenty-five. After the beneficiary reaches the age of twenty-five, we would continue to distribute all of the income from the trust. When the beneficiary reaches the age of thirty, we give the beneficiary the rest of the trust principal and terminate the trust.

It may well be that the only thing the beneficiary has left of the first distribution at age thirty is the wrecked Corvette and not enough money to fix it, but he or she may have learned something. Perhaps, when the money from the first distribution was gone, all of the new friends were also gone. If the amount of the trust principal is very large or the judgment of the beneficiary is questionable, we might make a distribution of one-fourth of the principal at age twenty-five, a second distribution of one-third of the principal at age thirty, and a final distribution of the remainder of the trust principal at age thirty-five.

In some cases, the people who set up the trust do not want to distribute the principal to the beneficiary. They want the principal distributed to the beneficiary's children after the beneficiary's death. In other cases, they want to keep the trust going until their deaths.

For example, grandmother and grandfather may be willing to make annual gifts to a grandchild's trust as long as the grandchild does not invade the principal without their advice and permission to do so. The grandchild knows that if he or she does invade the principal, the annual gifts from his or her grandparents will terminate. The grandparents may want the entire principal to be distributed at the death of the second of them, or they may want periodic distributions to begin upon the event of their deaths.

The IRC specifies that in order for a gift to qualify for the annual exclusion, the gift must be of a *present interest*. The case of *Crummey v Commissioner*, 397 F.2d 82 (9th Cir. 1968) is the criterion of whether or not a payment into a savings trust satisfies this requirement. This case holds that if the beneficiary can demand that he or she receive payment of gifts to the trust, the gift to the trustee constitutes a gift of a present interest. The power to make such a demand spelled out in a trust instrument is known as a *Crummey Power.*

If the beneficiary of the trust is a minor, we are presented with a special problem. The IRC states that in order for a gift to a trust for the benefit of a minor to be of a present interest, the trustee must either distribute the current income each year or distribute the principal when the minor attains the age of twenty-one years. Some adult must make the demand or decline to make the demand for distribution of the income and the annual gift to the trust on behalf of the minor.

If the child's parents set up the trust, someone other than the child's parents should have the power to make or refuse to make the demand. We can do this by having a *guardian* or *conservator* appointed for the child for purposes of this trust, depending on what such a person is called in a particular state. The sole function of the guardian or conservator is to decline to make the demand on behalf of the child.

Another section of the IRC comes into play at this point and presents a second problem if the trust has more than one present beneficiary. If a beneficiary declines to make the demand for a contribution to or income from the trust, that beneficiary has allowed a *power of appointment* over the property to have *lapsed.*

Under the IRC, by declining to demand the property, the beneficiary has made a gift to all of the other beneficiaries of the trust because he or she will have allowed a power of appointment to lapse. This gift is then deducted from the beneficiary's $600,000 lifetime total of gifts which he or she can make without incurring liability under the gift and estate tax. However, the IRC permits a beneficiary to decline the greater of $5,000 or 5% of the property over which the beneficiary enjoys a power of withdrawal without making a taxable gift.

If the total of the annual gift and the income does not exceed $5,000, or if there is only one beneficiary of the trust, there is no problem of lapsed power of appointment. However, we do not want to place a $5,000 per-beneficiary limit on persons who establish savings trusts with several beneficiaries. In order to utilize the "five and five" exception, we can draft Crummey Powers which limit the beneficiary's *power to decline to withdraw* to $5,000 or 5% of the property over which the beneficiary enjoys a power of withdrawal.

There are presently four versions of Crummey Powers which attorneys commonly use, three of which specify a "five and five" provision.

1. Hanging Crummey Powers. The attorney uses these powers when there is a substantial contribution at the time the trust is established, and the persons who set up the trust do not intend to continue making large contributions to the trust. The scheme will also work with continuing annual contributions, particularly where the beneficiaries are dependable. **Caveat**: Some attorneys are uncomfortable with hanging powers.

   a. Each year the trustee notifies each beneficiary that during the next sixty (60) days he or she has the right to withdraw his or her pro rata share of any property transferred to the trust.

   b. The amount of the withdrawal right for any individual will not exceed the amount of the annual exclusion which is permitted plus the amount of earlier rights of withdrawal which have not lapsed.

   c. The beneficiary's right of withdrawal will *lapse* to the extent of $5,000 or 5% of the property over which the beneficiary enjoys a power of withdrawal.

   d. The beneficiary's right of withdrawal will continue to lapse in a similar manner in subsequent years when the beneficiary does not exercise his or her right within sixty (60) days of notice, until the right has lapsed completely.

2. Cumulative Crummey Powers. This is a simple answer to the lapse problem. The power of withdrawal never does lapse. When the beneficiaries receive complete distribution of the trust

assets, the question of a lapsed power of appointment becomes moot. This can work well when the beneficiaries of the trust are mature.

a. Each year the trustee notifies each beneficiary that he or she has the right to withdraw his or her pro rata share of any property transferred to the trust.

b. The right of withdrawal of each beneficiary is cumulative and may be exercised at any time in the future.

c. If the beneficiary exercises the right prior to the time of final distribution of all of the trust assets, the trustee can distribute cash, other property, or insurance policies to satisfy the demand.

3. Special Testamentary Powers of Appointment. Attorneys who are uncomfortable with hanging powers sometimes use this method. The entire trust assets are ultimately distributed according to the terms of the trust and the question of the unlapsed right of withdrawal becomes moot. This system utilizes a section of the IRC which provides that a power of appointment has not lapsed if the holder of the power can appoint at his or her death.

a. Each year the trustee notifies each beneficiary that during the next sixty (60) days he or she has the right to withdraw his or her pro rata share of any property transferred to the trust.

b. The amount of the withdrawal right for any individual will not exceed the amount of the annual exclusion which is permitted.

c. The beneficiary's right of withdrawal will *lapse* to the extent of $5,000 or 5% of the property over which the beneficiary enjoys a power of withdrawal.

d. The beneficiary will not have a right of withdrawal on the portion which has not lapsed and this amount will accumulate, but the beneficiary can appoint, in his or her will or living trust, a beneficiary or beneficiaries from among his or her descendants or other beneficiaries under the trust agreement.

4. Crummey Powers Subject to "5 and 5" Limits. An attorney would use this method primarily when no annual gift from the insured will exceed $5,000 per beneficiary per year.

a. Each year the trustee notifies each beneficiary that during the next sixty (60) days he or she has the right to withdraw his or her pro rata share of the property transferred to the trust.

b. If a beneficiary does not exercise the power of withdrawal, it shall lapse with respect to the property covered by the notice.

c. The amount of the withdrawal right for any individual will not exceed $5,000 or 5% of the aggregate value of the assets out of which, or the proceeds out of which, the exercise of the lapsed powers could be satisfied.

You can establish a savings trust for an adult or for a child. If you wish the savings trust to be a tool of instruction as well as a vehicle for making gifts, it is best to have only one beneficiary of the trust. This means that you should establish a separate trust for each person to whom you wish to make periodic gifts, if you wish to exercise management over the gifts after you have made them. In this way, if you wish to stop making gifts to one beneficiary and continue making gifts to the others, you have the means to do so.

If your estate will not be subject to the Federal Gift and Estate Tax, you need not concern yourself with Crummey Powers in the trust. However, if your estate has exposure to this tax, you can see how it is far less difficult to satisfy the Crummey requirements if there is only one beneficiary of the trust.

If the sole beneficiary of the trust is a responsible adult, it may be easier to make the $10,000 gift to the adult and have the adult make a $10,000 contribution to the savings trust of which he or she is the sole beneficiary.

For large estates, this type of trust not only reduces the tax imposed upon the estate, but it avoids the tax on the gift and avoids the generation-skipping tax on gifts made to grandchildren who are present beneficiaries.

CHAPTER 14

The Irrevocable Life Insurance Trust

LIFE INSURANCE OFFERS a different type of solution to two problems presented by the tax imposed upon very large estates. These are as follows:

First, if the proceeds from an insurance policy on the life of a deceased, payable to the children of the deceased, are as large as the tax which will be imposed upon the estate, the children of the deceased will receive the same net amount as they would if the tax were not imposed.

Second, if the estate does not have sufficient cash to pay the tax, the proceeds from the life insurance can provide this cash at the time it will be needed. If necessary, the beneficiaries of the life insurance can lend money to the estate so that the estate will not find it necessary to sell assets at a time when they will not bring a good price.

The benefits of life insurance as an estate-planning tool are enhanced by the interesting treatment of the proceeds from life insurance under both the income tax sections and the gift and estate tax sections of the IRC.

First, if the insured person or persons retains *no incidents of ownership* in a policy of life insurance upon his or her life, neither the value of the policy nor the proceeds from the policy will be included in his or her estate for estate tax purposes. This is logical.

It is very important that the insured person does not retain such powers as the right to borrow against the policy or change the beneficiaries. As a rule of thumb, if the insured has no more rights than he or she would have had if someone else had purchased the policy, the incidents of ownership rule will be satisfied and the proceeds from the life-insurance policy will not be included in the insured's estate for estate tax purposes.

Second, the proceeds from life insurance are not taxed to the recipient as income. This is somewhat more difficult to justify. The proceeds from the life-insurance policy will be more than the premiums paid on the policy. There would appear to be gain on the entire transaction which could be subject to income tax. There are reasons for not imposing income tax upon these proceeds, but we won't go into them here.

There are two simple ways to take advantage of the unique tax characteristics of life insurance.

First, the insured person can purchase a life-insurance policy and then transfer all incidents of ownership in the policy to his or her children. If the value of the gift is less than the annual exclusion of $10,000 per person, it will escape the federal gift tax. However, if the transfer is made within three years of the insured's death, the IRC will classify it as a *transfer in anticipation of death* and bring the proceeds from the policy back into the estate for tax purposes.

Second, the insured person or persons can make a gift which qualifies for the annual exclusion to his or her children, and the children can purchase an insurance policy on the life of their parent or parents. This procedure avoids the danger of an incomplete transfer of all of the incidents of ownership in the policy.

These simple solutions work fine if all the children are mature, financially responsible, and get along with each other. However, often the children are young—perhaps even minors. The problems presented by the presence of young or irresponsible beneficiaries, or the presence of beneficiaries who do not get along well together, indicate the need for a trust.

There is the ever-present spectre of divorce with young people. If the insured's child owns the insurance policy, the value of the policy is property which would be considered in the event of a divorce settlement. Estate-planning attorneys have developed the *Irrevocable Life Insurance Trust* to address these problems.

There is probably no other type of estate-planning trust which is affected by as many sections of the IRC as the Irrevocable Life Insurance Trust. There are pitfalls present at every turn which could expose the attorney and the insurance people to very large liabilities. However, if we understand the requirements which the IRC imposes upon the insurance plan, and if we meet these requirements one step at a time in preparing the trust, we can utilize this valuable tool safely.

The estate-planning attorney constructs a life-insurance trust out of building blocks. Each of these blocks must accomplish the client's purpose in establishing the trust arrangement and must comply with the applicable sections of the IRC in order for the plan to receive the desired tax treatment. In my opinion, there is no question which the estate-planning attorney can face in trust preparation which is more complex or in which the attorney must satisfy as many sections of the tax law.

In the March 1985 edition of the *Journal of Taxation*, James G. Blase wrote an article entitled "Structuring Life Insurance Trusts to Avoid Estate Tax Inclusion Under Section 2035." The IRC states that any transfers made within three years of death will be included in the decedent's estate for estate tax purposes. Section 2035 deals with transfers from the deceased which were not made within three years of death. The following recommendations are among those which Mr. Blase made in his article to avoid having the value of life insurance held by an Irrevocable Life Insurance Trust included in the value of the estate of the deceased:

1. The trustee should not be required under the terms of the trust instrument to pay policy premiums.
2. The terms of the trust should not require that the insured contribute funds to the trust.
3. Any notation on the decedent-insured's check to the trustee to the effect that the funds are to be used to pay insurance premiums should be avoided.
4. The payment of insurance premium(s) should never exhaust the available liquid assets of the trust nor should the amount of the contribution be equal to the amount of the premium.

5. The drafter should be careful to include provisions in the trust instrument which allow or permit the trustee to distribute the net income of the trust during the insured's lifetime to someone other than the insured to avoid the inference that there is no purpose to the trust during the insured's lifetime other than the maintenance of an insurance policy on his life.

6. To the extent possible, contributions to the trust should be made far in advance of the actual premium payments by the trustee.

7. If possible, the trustee should not be someone over which the insured has the ability to exert control.

8. The trust instrument should always allow the trustee maximum discretion over trust investments.

9. The trust instrument itself should avoid any reference to the fact that it is intended to be an insurance trust and the title of the trust should not include the word *insurance*.

Under Mr. Blase's recommendations, the opening paragraph of the trust agreement should recite that some person or a couple has established this trust by an agreement with an independent trustee. The natural candidate to be such a trustee is a trust company or the trust department of a bank. Some corporate trustees will charge a nominal annual fee to serve in this capacity for an irrevocable life insurance if the trustee's duties are very limited until the time when the trustee is required to collect and distribute the proceeds from the life-insurance policy. The trustee's fee can be as low as $250 per year during the life of the insured.

The settlor(s), grantor(s), or donor(s) (person(s) who established the trust) should not retain the right to change trustees. The retention of that power could be interpreted as enough control over the trustee to have retained some incidents of ownership. However, we can give the beneficiary or beneficiaries of the trust the right to change trustees, perhaps by majority vote.

If the trust is drafted with an independent trustee and the remainder of Mr. Blase's recommendations are covered in the body of the instrument, we will have accomplished one of our objectives. The life insurance will not be included in the estate of the deceased-insured.

The second objective may be to have the gifts to the insurance trust excluded from the gift tax. Here again, we must use the same Crummey Powers as in the children's savings trust and make the same provision for a guardian for any minor children of the donor or donors.

Once we have satisfied all of the requirements of the IRC in such a

69

manner that: (1) the gifts from the insured to the trust are eligible for the annual exclusion; (2) the beneficiaries of the trust will receive the insurance proceeds without incurring income tax; and (3) the beneficiaries will have no adverse gift tax consequences because of having declined to exercise their right of withdrawal, we can structure the remainder of the trust to provide for management of the insurance proceeds after the death of the insured.

Here again, we do not want to pay a large sum of money to a young person, and certainly not to a minor. We put a scheme of distribution into the trust document similar to that which we would use in a living trust. The trust contains a provision stating that after the death of the donor or donors, the trustee has the power to lend money to any other trust with the same beneficiaries and the same scheme of distribution. This can provide the cash to finance the estate tax during the time when property in the donor's living trust is being liquidated.

The Irrevocable Life Insurance Trust is one of the most valuable tools available to the estate-planning community for very large estates. However, there are so many requirements imposed upon the trust by various sections of the IRC that the path to successful compliance is fraught with open pits into which the unwary can fall. A careful analysis of the client's needs and a careful drafting of the trust agreement will provide the client with a valuable estate-planning product.

CHAPTER 15

The Charitable Remainder Trust

A CHARITABLE REMAINDER trust is an agreement which a person (or a couple) as donor (or donors—persons making a gift) makes with a trustee. Under the agreement, the trustee agrees to manage funds and pay the donor a percentage of the value of the funds each year. The donor can specify that the payments continue to his (or her) children, upon the death of the donor. When all of the beneficiaries have died, the trustee pays the funds to a charity or charities which the donor has specified during his lifetime.

This particular type of charitable trust is specifically authorized under Section 664 of the IRC (IRC 664). The code section tells that the percentage of the value of the funds which the trustee pays to the donor, or his children, each year must be at least 5%, and the period during which the trustee makes the payments can be for the life of specific persons who are alive at the time the trust is signed or for a specific period not to exceed 20 years.

If the charity or charities who will receive the ultimate gift qualify under IRC 170, the donor receives a charitable deduction for the gift to the trust at the time he makes it. As with all charitable deductions, the donor is permitted a deduction of 50% or 30% of his taxable income, depending on the type of charity, and can carry the deduction forward for a period not to exceed 5 years.

However, the amount of the deduction allowed to a charitable remainder trust is reduced to reflect the fact that the donor has reserved income for a period of time. The chart below shows typical percentages for persons who have reserved income for life.

	INCOME YIELD*		
Age	5.0%	6.0%	7.0%
40	20.62%	15.78%	12.29%
45	25.10	19.86	15.93
50	30.23	24.66	20.35
55	35.94	30.14	25.52
60	42.21	36.33	31.51
65	48.85	43.06	38.16
70	55.83	50.31	45.51

* As a percent of the market value of the trust each year.

The trust will not work with an extremely small gift. The funds in the trust must be adequate to generate an income which is sufficient to make the payments to the donor and pay the trustee to manage the funds in the trust. The percentage of annual yield must not be so large as to make the payment schedule impractical, but could be as large as 10%. The gift should not be so large that the donor cannot use the entire charitable deduction in 5 years. Here we have a potential pitfall. The charitable deduction, in conjunction with other deductions which the donor may have, could trigger the application of the alternate minimum tax!

The main application of this type of trust involves making a gift of appreciated property. For example, if the donor has an asset with a fair market value which is far greater than his basis in the asset, he can make a gift of the asset to the trust, the trustee can sell the asset without paying any tax on the gain upon sale, and the donor can take a charitable deduction in the amount of the fair market value of the asset.

If the asset, such as a common stock, is paying a relatively small dividend which gives the donor an income of $20,000 per year, he might be able to receive two or three times the income during his lifetime, take a charitable deduction for the gift, and still make an important gift to a charity whose aims he wishes to advance.

Another possibility is for the donor to give part of the appreciated asset to the trust and receive enough of a charitable deduction to pay the tax he will incur upon his sale of the remainder of the asset.

The donor can name a family foundation which he has created as the ultimate beneficiary of the charitable remainder trust. The foundation can pay a reasonable salary to your family members who serve as directors of the trust and can carry out the donor's charitable aims.

The family foundation is an attractive option for those with large estates, for the gift made to the foundation is outside the donor's estate for estate tax purposes. This means that the estate tax is reduced by 55% of the amount of the gift made to the foundation. A substantial gift can do some very important things and still provide the donor's family members with very handsome directors' fees.

Perhaps the donor does not want to decrease the size of his estate. In certain cases, particularly with younger donors, it is sometimes possible to purchase a whole-life insurance policy in the amount of the gift with part of the proceeds from the trust payments. The donor would then create an insurance trust for the benefit of his children. The insurance trust would own the insurance policy, and the proceeds upon the donor's death would be tax free to the beneficiaries. In the case of a large estate, the amount of the face value of the policy would only have to be one-half of the amount of the gift to the charitable remainder trust in order to yield the donor's children the same amount, because of the estate-tax avoidance.

Perhaps you can give a charity the money you want to use to fund some child's or children's education. In order to do this, you would fund a charitable remainder trust and direct the trustee to pay up to $10,000 per year ($20,000 if you and your spouse are the donors of the charitable remainder trust) of the proceeds from the trust to you as trustee or trustees of a child's savings trust. As trustees of the savings trust, you would invest in growth investments until such time as the child is ready for college, thus avoiding income tax until the child needs the money.

You can draft a charitable remainder unitrust in such a manner that the trustee is to accrue the payments to you if there is inadequate income. You can then instruct the trustee, which can be you, to invest in growth investments. In such a case, any growth in excess of the income which you have reserved will serve to make the accrued payments larger.

Another possibility would be to direct the trustee of a charitable remainder unitrust to accrue payments until the beneficiary's death or until the beneficiary directs the trustee to make the accrued payments. This would permit additional discretion in the selection of investment vehicles.

Any asset, even cash, is suitable for a charitable remainder trust, if the donor wants to make a charitable gift upon his death. He gets the charitable deduction during his lifetime and the charity still gets the gift upon his death.

A person who is selling his business may want to give part of the stock to a charitable remainder trust prior to the sale and have the trust sell its stock at the same time as the donor sells his stock. The charitable deduction can offset part of the taxes on the donor's gain on sale of his stock, and the donor can receive a reasonable income from the funds in the charitable remainder trust for his lifetime, and the lifetime of his children, if he wishes.

Most commonly, the asset which the donor places in a charitable remainder trust is a stock which he bought at $10 per share and which is currently selling at $200 per share. However, the stock is a growth stock at a time when the donor wants income. If he sells the stock to buy something which will pay a higher yield, he will pay tax on the gain upon sale of $60 per share. Instead, he gives the stock to the charitable remainder trust.

The trustee sells the stock and pays no tax upon the gain. The trust puts the proceeds of the sale into a high-yield investment, and the donor receives a yield of 10% on his investment for life.

The charity gets funding, thus advancing a public policy. The government will get its taxes, and normally more taxes, over the lifetime of the donor. The funds in the charitable remainder trust will be invested and finance the commerce of the country. Perhaps it's done with mirrors.

CHAPTER 16

Physical Disability and the Nursing Home

A MAJOR ILLNESS can be devastating to anyone who does not have rather complete medical insurance coverage. We become more concerned with this problem as our age advances. Congress enacted a statute which provided for federal catastrophic health insurance, but it was so unpopular that it was repealed shortly after enactment.

Many people in their declining years also fear that they will be confined to a nursing home and their savings will be exhausted. We do not want our spouse to become destitute, and we want our savings to remain intact and passed along to our children. If you think about the circumstances under which people you've known have died, you will find that only a small percentage of them spent much time in the hospital during their final illness and only a small percentage of them spent a long time in a nursing home. However, our fears persist even in the face of all the facts.

Our state and federal-assistance programs are designed so that people who have spent their lives as freeloaders of society can be confined to a nursing home and receive this service without charge from the first day. On the other hand, people who have worked all their lives and saved for their declining years must pay for this service until they finally become destitute and lack any means to pay. Only then will we treat them as well as we treat the freeloaders.

There are several ways for our noble and productive seniors to approach this dilemma. Most of these schemes don't work very well, and there is a disadvantage to each of them. All of these schemes are designed to impoverish the person who needs social assistance. None of these schemes will yield any benefit to someone who never does spend a great deal of time in a nursing home.

You must first understand how you go about making the government pay for nursing-home care before you can understand the various ways you can keep the government from taking all your money. You can find out what the requirements are in your particular state by examining the form you must fill out in order to receive the social assistance. You can get a copy of this form from the office of almost any nursing home.

You will find that the state will not take your personal residence as long as you are alive. The state wants you to get better and go back home. Most states will not take your residence after your death. The state will probably not take your tangible personal property at any time. You will be permitted to keep a certain amount of savings and an automobile of a certain value. You will be permitted to pay for your funeral in advance. Any funeral home can tell you exactly where you stand on this matter. However, the state will recover any gifts which you made recently. There will be a question on the application form asking whether you have made any gifts within the last 30 months. This figure of 30 months varies from state to state and it keeps changing. Remember, the laws keep changing!

Any law which rewards people who have acted contrary to our public policy of having people work hard, save for their declining years, and keep control of their property for their entire lives is severely flawed. The law which affects the matters which we are discussing has an even more serious flaw in it. For example, if husband is expected to go into a nursing home in the future and wife is in good health, they can get a divorce and have all of the marital property go to wife, leaving husband destitute. When husband goes into the nursing home, the state will pay for everything and the family assets are protected from the state. This scheme is the least commonly used of all of the ways to avoid the confiscation.

You can simply spend all of the money on things which the state will not confiscate. If the state will not take the furniture, you can buy all new furniture for your home. If the state will not take jewelry or art work, you can buy jewelry or art work. If the state will not take the home, you can remodel it.

Most people really get serious about protecting their property during the time when one of their children is paying all of their bills with their money and driving them to religious functions. They decide that they would like to give their property away and still have the use of it. There is no way that this can actually be done. When you give something away, it no longer belongs to you and you can make no claim upon it.

The *Grantor Retained Income Trust* comes as close to accomplishing this as anything you might do. However, the state will take all of your income, even after you have applied for assistance and have entered the nursing home, if you use this system. If you have transferred your property into this trust more than 30 months before entering the nursing home, or whatever the waiting period is, you can apply for the state to pay for your nursing home expenses at the time you enter. However, if you enter a nursing home only one year after you transferred your property, you will have to pay your own way for 18 months before you apply for assistance or the state will take the assets in your Grantor Retained Income Trust. The state will do this because you made the gift less than 30 months before asking for the assistance. Under the terms of the trust, you have a right to the income, but nobody has a right to invade the principal in order to pay for the nursing home for 18 months.

There is a scheme which may be practical for you if you have a very close family which is not prone to greed. We call this a *Family Trust*. Your child, or children, establish a trust in which they are the settlors. One of your children is the trustee. This is usually the child who is assisting you in your financial affairs at the time you decide to do something to protect your property. Under the terms of the trust, the trustee can pay any amount of income and principal to anyone the trustee deems appropriate, other than to the trustee or the settlors. Your name will not appear anywhere in the trust.

You transfer all of your property into the Family Trust. Your child, the trustee, pays all of your bills and gives you whatever amount you want to spend on yourself. If you go into a nursing home before the required waiting period, the trustee pays for the nursing home until the waiting period has expired. Remember, the law keeps changing and the waiting period which applies to you may change at some time in the future.

Your child applies for the state to pay for the nursing home once the waiting period has expired. The trustee still has money to give you for whatever you want for the rest of your life. The trust calls for complete or partial distribution of the trust property when a majority of the settlors vote to do this. It may be that the trust assets are far in excess of any foreseeable need which you may have. At that time, the settlors would vote for a partial distribution of the excess property in the trust.

When you, or you and your spouse, die, the settlors will vote for complete distribution of the trust property. The scheme of distribution will be the scheme of distribution which you would put in your will.

Any scheme which you use to avoid the cost of catastrophic health problems or the nursing home will be "the lesser of two evils" at best. Keep control of your property for the rest of your life! However, if you determine that the confiscatory effects of our statutes are a greater evil than the loss of control of your property, you can use one of the schemes which we have described here. Think twice! If your estate is large enough to pay for these expenses, we suggest that you not worry.

There are insurance policies available to pay for nursing-home care for a certain period of time. If you have such a policy which would pay for care during the waiting period, you could transfer your assets at the time you enter the nursing home and make application for the state to pay at the time the policy payments terminated. However, you may not be competent to make gifts at the time you enter the nursing home. If you have not made proper provision for this while you are competent, there is no way you will be able to make gifts pursuant to a court order.

Some of these insurance policies are very expensive. It is a business decision as to whether the insurance will represent a long-term savings to your estate. Some policies require you to be hospitalized a certain number of days before entering the nursing home. If there is no reason to send you into the hospital, you may not have nursing-home coverage. Examine the terms of the insurance policy carefully and ask for references from people who have had nursing home care paid for under this policy.

CHAPTER 17

The Second Home

In MANY FAMILIES, there is a place where the family gathers during holidays for recreation and companionship. This may be a cottage "at the lake," or it may be the winter home which the parents occupy in Florida, Arizona, or Texas. In many cases, the parents would like this home to remain "in the family" for the enjoyment of the heirs.

Many of the schemes which people have used for this purpose have yielded results which fall far short of their objectives. The problem is very much like that faced by the group of unrelated persons who want to have a hunting or fishing camp which will continue through the generations of those who built the camp. The traditional way of solving this problem was to form a not-for-profit corporation in which the various members would hold stock. In almost every case, as one generation passed on, the next generation would sell the stock to persons with very little association with the original group. The result was that the people who had a right to use the facility did not want to be there at the same time because they did not enjoy the company of the other shareholders.

You can use a corporate form with restrictions on the transfer of shares to keep the facilities within a family, provided the other family shareholders have both the willingness and financial ability to purchase shares, which would otherwise pass outside the family.

If you have a residence or a cottage which you want your lineal descendants to use after you are gone, there is a way in which you can accomplish your aims. You can establish a *Recreational Home Trust*. This is nothing more than a living trust in which you, or you and your spouse, retain complete control of the recreational property as long as you live. You convey the recreational home to yourself or yourselves as trustee or trustees of this trust. You also convey enough income-producing securities into the trust to pay the taxes, maintenance, and utilities for the recreational home. Upon your death, or upon the death of the second of you, the successor trustee maintains the home for the benefit of your heirs.

Problems can develop which you cannot possibly foresee. For example, if your daughter dies leaving living children, her interest should pass to her children, not her husband. We do not want her widower to take her interest, remarry, die, and have her interest pass to his new wife and her five rowdy children. A provision in the trust which would preclude this is relatively easy to draft.

It is also possible for one of your children, or some of your grandchildren, to become an irritation to the rest of the family. When this occurs, the other family members may not want to use the place. We can construct a trust document which provides for the rights of your family with respect to the use of the home. There must also be a mechanism under which a majority of your family can pay an objectionable member for his or her share or terminate the trust and distribute the proceeds.

Always think twice before you decide to rule from the grave for a prolonged period of time. There must be a mechanism under which your family can terminate their interest in the recreational home.

Do not even consider deeding the property to your children. If you do such a thing, you invite a court action which could cost as much as the second home itself is worth. It is possible that a corporate scheme could solve this problem, but I have yet to see a corporate scheme which has the flexibility or control which a trust can provide.

We might ask, "Who should be the successor trustee?" If the child to whom you would look as the successor of your living trust or trusts is a resident of the immediate area of your second home, you might consider having him or her serve as successor trustee. However, the position of successor trustee of such a trust is going to be criticized no matter what may happen in the future. If you have no children who live in the same area as the second home, or if any child which you might have is very active in business endeavors, appoint a corporate successor trustee. The only duties of the trustee will be to invest the money, pay the bills, and count the votes on any rules of use or agreement for disposition.

CHAPTER 18

The Toy Trust

IF YOU DECIDE to have a bank or trust company act as the trustee of your living trust, that corporation may not want to have you transfer your airplane, snow machine, power boat, or real estate to its name. The problem is that of liability.

The trust officer of a large Detroit bank recounted the story of his succeeding to the trusteeship of a large trust which counted many parcels of land among its assets. The abstract of one parcel read, "formerly known as 'The Old Dump Site.'" Certain environmental laws now require the person "now holding title to the land" to pay the cost of cleaning the environment. We do not wish to discuss the moral questions of whether or not a person should be required to pay for damage which he or she did not cause; we only wish to point out that this has now become a problem.

Attorneys create a separate living trust to handle these assets. They will generally refer to such a trust as a "personal trust" or a "toy trust," because this is where you place your adult toys. This trust can have a second purpose. Perhaps the income from your primary trust is more than adequate to support you, and you wish to invest the remainder of the income in something more risky than the corporate trustee might buy. You are the trustee of this trust and the powers which you hold as trustee are such that you can bet the entire assets on the horses if you wish.

The terms of a personal trust permit you to do anything you want to do with the property in the trust as long as you, or you and your spouse, remain among the living. Upon your death, or upon the death of you and your spouse, all of the assets of this trust pour into your main trust so that they will be distributed in accordance with your wishes.

The successor of your toy trust should be the same as the successor of your living trust. This facilitates the transfer of assets. Even in your toy trust you can use the services of a financial advisor or corporate trustee acting as an agent. If you talk to your financial advisors or your corporate trustees, they can tell you how this works.

CHAPTER 19

The Person Receiving Disability Benefits

IN MANY CASES, a disabled person may be entitled to receive governmental benefits of a monetary value far beyond anything that person's family could afford. The disability may be a mental impairment or mental illness, or it may be a physical affliction that makes it difficult for the person to obtain employment which provides an adequate income. The disabled person may require constant care at certain times.

The criteria which the governmental agency uses to determine whether or not a person is eligible for assistance include the person's ability to pay for the necessary services. Unfortunately, someone can have resources which disqualify him or her from the assistance and yet have inadequate resources to pay for the services for which the government would pay.

You must begin by finding out what a disabled person may *own* and still be eligible for the entitlements. This list will vary from state to state. You must determine what the law is in your state. You will probably find that a disabled person can have: (1) a certain amount of cash; (2) an automobile which does not exceed a certain value; (3) furniture, clothing, jewelry, and appliances, with no limitation on their value; and (4) a home without limitation on its value.

CAVEAT: In some states, the government may levy upon the disabled person's home after his or her death. If the disabled person owns property which would disqualify him or her, he or she can give the property to someone else.

The secret to receiving a governmental entitlement is to become poor and then to remain poor. The application for the entitlement will contain a question as to whether you made any gifts during the previous 30 months or some other period. You must arrange things in such a manner that any transfers occur prior to the beginning of this waiting period.

You can have nice furnishings, a state-of-the-art stereo system, and a beautiful television set and still qualify for your entitlements. Someone can hire a cleaning service for your apartment and pay for the taxis which you need without disqualifying you.

Loving parents may want to provide money so that a disabled son or daughter can enjoy a better life. The problem which they face is that the money which they provide could disqualify their child from receiving the necessary governmental assistance.

There are many things which you can do for your disabled child or give to your disabled child without disqualifying your child from entitlements. For example, if the criterion for money is a particular sum such as $1,000, be certain the child does not have more than that amount of money at any time. If the criterion for an automobile is one worth a certain amount of money, don't buy an automobile for your child which is worth more than that amount. You can see the pattern here. Be certain that the disabled person's possessions do not disqualify him or her.

It is easy to provide and buy with care as long as you are alive. The problems arise when you decide to set aside money to provide for your disabled child after you are gone. If the child *has a right* to receive money, the child has an asset which could disqualify him or her.

Traditionally, our public policy has required people to exhaust their resources before they can be entitled to governmental assistance. This policy appears to be changing. You cannot, and you will probably never be able to, put property into a trust which you establish for your own benefit and avoid having this property considered in an application for public assistance. The reason for this is simple. You would have done nothing more than make a gift to yourself and you still have a right to receive the benefits. However, you can set up a trust for the benefit of your disabled child in such a manner that the child is still eligible for governmental entitlements. The trust must be what attorneys refer to as a *Spendthrift Trust*. These trusts originated for use with children who "couldn't handle money." Most trusts which are established for the benefit of others now contain such a provision. The following is an example:

ARTICLE X
Spendthrift Provision

Except as otherwise provided in this agreement, no beneficiary may assign, pledge, sell, transfer, or encumber his or her interest, in any manner, nor may any beneficiary anticipate any payments of principal or income payable, or to become payable, to the beneficiary under any trust created under this agreement, nor shall that interest, while in the possession of the Trustee, be liable for or subject to the debts, contracts, obligations, liabilities, or torts of any beneficiary.

The spendthrift provision precludes the beneficiary from *anticipating* the benefits which he or she may receive from the trust. This means that the beneficiary cannot assign the benefits, and the trustee will pay the benefits to the beneficiary directly even if the beneficiary tries to assign them. The trustee cannot be required to pay anything to the government.

The terms of the trust give the trustee broad discretion to "distribute income and principal from the trust to the beneficiary or for the benefit of the beneficiary." The terms of the trust specifically direct the trustee not to make any disbursement which would disqualify the beneficiary from receiving any governmental entitlements which could benefit him or her.

You can have money and property go into this trust from your living trust or will upon your death, or the spendthrift trust for the benefit of your disabled child can be part of your living trust. The problem of having the property go into the trust from the probate of your will is that the probate court may require annual reports from the trustee. This will cost money which could go to your child.

Eventually, your disabled child will die. The property which you have set aside for him or her could go to your child's spouse, your child's children, or it could go to someone else if your child does not have a spouse or children at the time of his or her death. The trust can be arranged in such a manner that it would take care of your child's spouse and children even if he or she is unmarried now.

Always keep your goals in sight. You wish to enrich your child's life and ease the burden which your child might impose upon others. You can direct that your home be put into the spendthrift trust, if there is some reason why the child might want to remain in that home. You can direct that the furnishings remain in the home. The trustee certainly has discretion to pay for taxes on the home, repairs and improvements to the home, and utilities such as electricity, water, and so forth. Be certain that the trustee is not *required* to pay for these, for your child would then have a right to receive this money and it could disqualify him or her.

It is within the trustee's discretion to pay for a cleaning service for the home and for someone to assist with meals and other needs which your particular child may have. The trustee would pay the provider of the service directly, rather than give the money to your child.

This is a developing area of estate planning. The provisions which give the trustee of the spendthrift trust the discretion to enhance the life of the disabled person should be specific enough that the trustee is comfortable with the disbursements which the trustee makes. As time goes on, attorneys will create trust provisions which are more specific and more easily understood by the trustees who must administer them. At present, there is room for improvement in the language which lawyers use. All good lawyers copy from other lawyers. When a lawyer sees something in a document which is better than what he or she is using, the lawyer will begin using the better language.

The following is an example of language which an attorney might use in the joint living trust for a couple with a small estate who has one disabled adult child receiving some sort of governmental entitlement:

ARTICLE VII

Distribution Upon the Death of the Settlors

Upon the death of the first Settlor to die, the surviving Settlor shall become the sole beneficial owner of the entire Trust Estate, to the same extent and with the same powers as if that Settlor were originally a sole Settlor and had funded the Trust with that Settlor's property, exclusively. Upon the death of both Settlors, the Trustee shall collect any insurance proceeds upon that occasion along with any property which may be added from the Settlors' general estates and shall hold, manage, and distribute the Trust Estate for the benefit of Charles C. Smith ("Charlie"), as set forth below, if he survives the Settlors. If he does not survive the Settlors and dies without leaving a spouse or issue then living, the Trustee shall distribute the Trust Estate to the Salvation Army of the City of East Overshoe, New Hampshire. If he does not survive the Settlors and leaves a spouse then living, the Trustee shall distribute the Trust Estate to his spouse, free of trust. If he does not survive the Settlors and leaves no spouse but does leave issue then living, the Trustee shall hold, manage, and distribute the Trust Estate for the benefit of the issue of Charlie, as set forth in Article VIII.

(1) The Trustee may pay to or apply for his benefit such sums from the interest and principal of the Trust Estate as in its sole discretion shall be necessary or advisable from time to time for Charlie's maintenance, medical care, and education, taking into consideration to the extent the Trustee deems advisable, any other income or sources of support for Charlie of which the Trustee knows, including any public assistance to which Charlie is entitled.

(2) The Trustee shall not reimburse or pay any governmental or charitable organization or agency for services which the Trustee deems to be adequate and which Charlie would enjoy at no cost if he were not the beneficiary of this trust.

(3) The Trustee shall make no disbursements which would render Charlie ineligible for any governmental or charitable entitlements which he is receiving at the time of the disbursement.

(4) The Settlors intend that the benefits from the Trust Estate be used to enrich Charlie's life and ease the burden which Charlie might impose upon others. The Trustee may, in its sole discretion, permit Charlie to occupy the Settlor's home and use the Settlor's furnishings and appliances. The Trustee may pay for taxes on the home, repairs and improvements to the home and utilities such as electricity, water, and other expenses of the home. It is within the Trustee's discretion to pay for a cleaning service for the home and for someone to assist with meals and other needs which Charlie may have from time to time.

(5) The Trustee shall be absolutely immune from any claim that it abused its discretion in making or refusing to make a disbursement for Charlie's benefit. In its discretion, the Trustee need only be of the opinion that loving parents who had set aside this Trust Estate to enrich Charlie's life and ease the burden which Charlie might impose upon others would have made the disbursement.

(6) Upon Charlie's death, the Trustee shall hold, administer, and distribute the Trust Estate as if Charlie had not survived the Settlors.

If you have several children and one of them is disabled, it might be a good idea to create a separate spendthrift trust for the disabled child and fund it upon your death by a gift from your living trust. In this way, you can set aside a certain amount of your estate for the child and distribute the remainder to your other children in the normal manner.

You might have one of your other children as trustee of the spendthrift trust, or you might select a corporate trustee. If you use one of your other children, it should be a child who has a close relationship to your disabled child and lives close to your child.

Sometimes the fees of a corporate trustee can be too high for it to manage a small trust. There are corporate trustees which specialize in small trusts, but you might not have one where you live. In certain areas, there are charitable organizations which will act as trustee for this type of spendthrift trust. Guardianship Advocacy Programs of New Jersey (GAP) offers such a service. If your area doesn't have one, perhaps you can help get one started.

Disability poses problems for both the disabled and the family of the disabled person. The public is becoming somewhat more understanding of the problems of the disabled. We have opened new areas of employment and are finding new treatments. You can do nothing more than advocate on behalf of your disabled child and make whatever provision for him or her that is within your means.

CHAPTER 20

Summary

WE HAVE WALTZED you through the minefield of estate planning and the gift and estate tax law. It might be well to look back on what we have said about the subject.

The services of an estate-planning attorney are the legal equivalent of preventive medicine. It is better to remain healthy than to go to the hospital and get cured. Likewise, it is better to stay out of court than to go to court and win. Stay away from people sitting on elevated benches wearing black robes! If you find yourself in court, stay close to your checkbook. You will be using it very often.

There are two facets to the services which an estate-planning attorney renders to clients. The first deals with the fact that any of us could become disabled and unable to make business or medical decisions. The second deals with the fact that all of us will die. Don't plan on dying soon, and don't plan on living forever. More often than you could imagine, attorneys do estate plans for people who do not expect to survive for more than a week and who get better. On the other hand, if we were never going to die, we could never think about retirement.

THE PROBLEM OF DISABILITY

Everyone needs three different types of documents to handle the problems which disability can pose. These are the power of attorney, the living will, and the power of attorney for medical care.

The Power of Attorney

A power of attorney is a document which appoints someone to be your attorney-in-fact. If the husband who was in a coma in the example in Chapter 9 had executed a durable power of attorney during the time when he was competent, it would have saved his wife a minimum of $2,100 for the probate court proceedings. Plan ahead and your family can stay away from people on elevated benches wearing black robes.

The Living Will

The living will takes care of the situation where you are in a coma and there is little hope that you will ever regain consciousness, no matter what your attending physician does. You can execute a document known as a Declaration to Physicians. Depending on your wishes, this document can direct your attending physicians to keep you hooked up to the machines even if your brain has ceased to function, or it can tell them to disconnect you from all but the feeding tubes. You can also direct that they disconnect you altogether and let you "die with dignity." This is your decision. However, if you do not wish to make the decision, your family can spend years in court trying to get permission to make the decision for you.

The Power of Attorney for Medical Care

If you are unable to give permission for medical care by reason of incompetence, you need a different type of document. This document is known as a Power of Attorney for Medical Care. If your attending physician and another physician agree that you are unable to handle your own affairs, the person designated in the document can make medical decisions for you. This document not only takes care of the problem when you are unconscious as the result of an automobile accident, it provides for someone to decide that you should be admitted to a nursing home for long-term care. In all of these situations, if you do not plan in advance, it will cost your family a great deal of money if they must go to court to get the authority which you could have granted with the stroke of a pen.

FINAL DISTRIBUTION OF YOUR PROPERTY

When you are no longer living, someone else will own everything which you now own. You show that you are the owner of things which are not registered in your name, such as your furniture and dishes, by possession. If you want to transfer ownership of something which is not registered in your name, you change possession of the object. This is true whether the transfer of ownership involves a sale or a gift. The law refers to this act as a delivery. If it is not convenient to deliver the object, you can do a symbolic delivery. We call this a Bill of Sale or a Deed of Gift.

If you want to change the ownership of something which is registered in your name, you have to sign some sort of paper. Land is always in someone's name, and you sign a deed. You sign the back of your car title and so forth. The question we face in estate planning is, "How do we sign these papers and make these deliveries when we are no longer living?" The law has devised four ways for you to handle this problem.

The Last Will and Testament

You can make a will. In your will you tell what you want done and name someone who will carry out your wishes. In the past, we referred to the person who was to carry out your wishes as your executrix or executor. We now call that person your personal representative. A will has no legal effect until two things happen. First, you have to die. You can make a new will as long as you are living and competent. Second, someone must take your will before the probate court.

Probate is a procedure in which a probate judge determines whether the will is valid. If the judge says the will is valid, the judge appoints someone to act as personal representative. Every family has a probate horror story which they can tell about a big probate fight after which family members no longer talk to each other. It took years to settle the estate and the lawyers got all the money. We would like to avoid probate. Remember, stay away from people on elevated benches who are wearing black robes!

Joint Ownership With Right of Survivorship

Second, you can place the things you own into joint ownership with someone else in such a way that the survivor becomes the owner. Never, under any circumstances whatsoever, place anything you own into joint ownership with anyone on the face of this earth, other than your spouse. There are many more joint-ownership horror stories than there are probate horror stories. Once you have put something into joint ownership, you cannot sell it without getting permission from the joint owner. You can sever the joint ownership and lose one-half of the property.

Joint ownership is a poor probate-avoidance scheme because everyone has to die in the right order to make the scheme work. Keep control of everything you own until the day you die!

Payable on Death

Third, you can make things payable on death to someone. Life insurance, your IRA, and many deferred compensation plans provide a death benefit. You can make your checking and savings accounts payable on death to someone. Series E Bonds can be made payable on death to someone. You can often, but not always, change the person to whom something is payable on death. To this extent, it is preferable to joint ownership where you are actually making a gift. However, everyone must still die in the right order to make the probate-avoidance scheme work.

The Living Trust

Fourth, you can create a living trust. This is the prime tool used in every proper estate plan, independent of the size of the estate. A living trust is an agreement, or a contract, which you make with yourself. You agree to hold all of your property as trustee for your own benefit. You specify, in your trust, what you want done with your property after your death. During your lifetime, you can do anything you want without getting permission from anyone.

From a practical viewpoint, the only difference between having a living trust and not having one is the way in which you title your property. For example, Al and Betty Smith would title their property in the name of "Alfred A. Smith and Betty B. Smith, Trustees of the

93

Alfred and Betty Smith Living Trust, dated such and such." If they have young children, they would name a corporate trustee as their successor trustee. When they die, the successor trustee steps into their shoes and becomes the trustee. All that the new trustee has to do to record a deed, for example, is to attach a copy of Al's death certificate and Betty's death certificate and a copy of the pages of their trust which name the successor trustee. If you put your car in someone's name and tell him to sell it, he can do so without going before any court. That is why there is no probate with a properly funded living trust.

THE FEDERAL GIFT AND ESTATE TAX

The federal government does not tax the person who receives a gift. However, the federal government taxes every gift which anyone makes during lifetime or upon death unless the gift falls under the $10,000 annual exclusion, qualifies for the unlimited marital deduction, or is a gift to a charitable organization. The Federal Gift and Estate Tax is structured in such a manner that each of us can gift away a total of $600,000 during our lifetime and at death.

If the total of everything you own plus the value of any life insurance which will come into your estate upon your death is less than $600,000, you need not concern yourself with this tax. Estate-planning attorneys refer to this as "a small estate." However, if your estate is $700,000, the federal government will take $37,000 that would otherwise go to your children. The marginal tax rate rises rather rapidly to over 50%.

Create Two Living Trusts

There are six basic ways to reduce or avoid the amount of tax which will be imposed upon a large estate. Simply by using living trusts, a married couple can avoid almost a quarter million dollars in estate tax. This is because each of them can pass $600,000 tax-free. By splitting the estate into his trust and her trust, they can pass $1,200,000 without paying any tax.

There is almost no disadvantage to this tax-avoidance scheme, even if this is a second marriage with one spouse having a great deal of money and the other spouse having very little. We can handle that by using a Qualified Terminal Interest Property Trust. Every other tax-avoidance scheme has some drawback to it.

Reduce the Size of the Estate

You can reduce the size of your estate by making annual $10,000 gifts to your children and grandchildren. These are not taxed and your estate will be reduced by the amount of the gift, but you will not have the money after you have made the gift.

The Irrevocable Life Insurance Trust

You can reduce the size of an estate and substitute payments to beneficiaries in the amount of the estate tax through the use of an Irrevocable Life Insurance Trust. You make gifts to a trust where your children are the beneficiaries. The trustee buys insurance on your life and makes it payable to the trust. The gifts are tax free, your estate is reduced by the amount of the gifts, and the trust does not pay any tax on the insurance proceeds when you die. The trustee of this trust can lend money to the trustee of your living trust when you die to finance the payment of your estate tax if there is property which should not be sold in a soft market. The trustee distributes the money to your children when all of the dust settles.

The Charitable Remainder Trust

You can reduce the size of your taxable estate by making charitable gifts during your lifetime or at death. If you are going to make these gifts upon the event of your death, you should create a Charitable Remainder Trust. By doing this, you can claim a charitable deduction from your taxable income this year and still receive the income from the donation. The charitable trust can sell appreciated property without paying any income tax and then invest the proceeds in securities with a higher yield.

The Grantor Retained Income Trust

You can reduce the value of the gifts which are taxed by creating a Grantor Retained Income Trust. These are trusts in which the person or couple who sets up the trust receives the income from or the use of the property which they put into the trust for a period, but makes a present gift of the future use of the property. This still creates a taxable gift, but the value of the gift is reduced. The tax is imposed only upon the present value of the future interest.

Freeze the Value of the Estate

Lastly, you can freeze the value of the estate by preventing the assets in the estate from increasing in value. If you own something which is virtually certain to increase in value, an attorney can structure an arrangement in which you will receive the present value of the asset in exchange for stock or money.

Your children will receive the asset itself and will receive the benefit of any increase in value. A Grantor Retained Income Trust does this to a certain extent, but that involves a presently taxable gift to your children. Generally, an estate freeze scheme does not.

SUMMARY

You might ask, "Why doesn't everyone do the things which you have recommended in this book?" We don't know. Perhaps everyone has not yet read the book. Clearly, we have recommended that you do certain specific things with respect to your affairs.

We recommend that you execute the appropriate powers of attorney, powers of attorney for medical care, and a living will. We hope that none of these documents are ever used. However, if you become incompetent and have not executed these documents, it will cost your family a great deal of money to go before the probate court.

We further recommend that you create a living trust and a pourover will, no matter how small your estate may be. If you are married and have an estate which has a fair market value of over $600,000, including any insurance which will pour into the estate upon your death, we recommend that both you and your spouse have a living trust and a pourover will in order to avoid the federal estate tax. We recommend that you transfer all of your property into your trust or trusts.

The idea that even a person with a small estate should have a complete estate plan is rather new. In the past, only the wealthy could afford the cost of preparing an estate plan. When you look at the sample estate-planning documents in the appendix, imagine how long it would take a secretary using a typewriter to prepare these documents—letter perfect!

The word processor has changed all this. Once an attorney has prepared a document which he or she thinks is well drafted, it can be put into memory and recalled for use in the future. There are computer programs available to attorneys which will prepare documents which are approximately what the attorney wants. Once the documents are in rough draft form, the attorney can edit them to bring them to the exact wording for the present client. The laser printer has helped. For example, it will print the documents in the appendix in this book in about ten minutes.

It is doubtful that the cost of preparing the documents for a complete estate plan will ever be less than it is presently. The price of a good computer and a good printer may come down somewhat, but the cost of operating a law office will not. Even though the end product of an estate-planning attorney's efforts is a set of documents, the attorney is selling his time, his knowledge, and his ingenuity. Whatever the attorney charges for preparing your estate plan, it will be less than the attorney fees you will encounter if you have not done what we have suggested in this book.

Finally, review your plan from time to time to be certain that it does what you presently want done. If there are changes in laws which affect your documents or your plans, be certain that you are in compliance with the current state of the law. If you suspect that a change in the law has some effect on your estate plan, contact your attorney.

Sample Estate-Planning Documents

IT IS VERY difficult for someone who has never seen a trust, will, or power of attorney to understand the ideas behind these documents. In this publication we have tried to do something akin to explaining the appearance of a camel to someone who has never seen one.

To assist you in your understanding of estate planning, we are including a set of sample documents similar to those which an attorney would send to clients after the initial interview. These are documents for fictitious clients named Alfred and Betty Smith. Al and Betty have an estate of about $200,000, plus life insurance of $300,000, and three children, two of whom are minors. These clients want to have complete control of their lives and property as long as they are alive, and they want to be sure that neither they nor their children will never have to go into court in the event of a medical tragedy.

Your attorney will probably include a cover letter with your draft documents which explains the documents. We are including a copy of a typical letter. Read the letter explaining the documents as you read the documents themselves. We are sure you will be able to understand how everything works after you have gone through the documents.

If you have a very large estate, the trusts in your split estate would include the additional provisions discussed in the chapter on this subject. For example, if Al and Betty had a $1,000,000 estate instead of an estate of $500,000, Article VII of the trust would direct the trustee to place as much as Al or Betty could give away without incurring any estate tax into a tax shelter, or Trust B, and place the remainder of the trust estate into the trust of the surviving spouse. Al's trust would state the following:

ARTICLE VII

Distribution After the Settlor's Death

Upon the death of the Settlor, the Trustee shall divide the Trust Estate (which shall include any property which may be added from the Settlor's general estate) as follows:

(1) If the Settlor is survived by his wife, Betty B. Smith, the Trustee shall divide the Trust Estate into Two (2) Shares which shall be known as Share A and Trust B. The Trustee shall select property of a sufficient value, taking into consideration any gifts which the Settlor may have made during his lifetime, to utilize the Settlor's entire unified credit under the provisions of IRC Section 2010 and place this property into Trust B. Share A shall be the remainder of the property in the Trust Estate. The Trustee shall pay Share A to Betty B. Smith, Trustee of the Betty B. Smith Living Trust dated December 7, 1991.

(2) If the Settlor's wife, Betty B. Smith, shall not survive him, Trust B shall be the entire Trust Estate.

(3) Notwithstanding anything contained in this agreement to the contrary, should the Settlor and his wife suffer a simultaneous death, the Trustee shall select sufficient property which qualifies under the provisions of IRC Section 2010 to equalize the Federal Estate Tax imposed upon the Settlor's estate and the Settlor's wife's estate and transfer this property to Northern Trust Bank of Florida/Naples N.A., Trustee of the Betty B. Smith Living Trust dated December 7, 1991, placing the remainder of the Trust Estate into Trust B.

Trust B shall be administered as set forth below.

Under the terms of this article, if Al predeceased Betty and had $700,000 worth of property in his trust at the time of his death, the trustee would transfer $100,000 into Betty's trust as a tax-free transfer and place $600,000 into Al's Trust B. You can see that there will never be any tax upon the estate of the first to die.

Article VIII of Al's trust would specify the use of Trust B during Betty's lifetime. This article gives Betty something which is very close to ownership, but falls enough short of complete ownership so that this property will not be taxed as part of Betty's estate when she dies. Betty not only gets all of the income from Trust B, but the trustee has discretion to invade the principal for Betty's "medical care, education, support, and maintenance in reasonable comfort." Betty would want to use the property in her own trust before invading Al's Trust B, because the taxes have been paid on Trust B and her trust could be exposed to the federal estate tax.

ARTICLE VIII

Provision for Settlor's Spouse During Lifetime

The Trustee shall hold, administer, and distribute Trust B as set forth below:

(1) Commencing with the date of the Settlor's death, the Trustee shall pay to or apply for the benefit of the Settlor's wife during her lifetime all the net income from Trust B in convenient installments but no less frequently than quarter-annually.

(2) In addition, the Trustee may pay to or apply for the benefit of the Settlor's wife such sums from the principal of Trust B as in her sole discretion shall be necessary or advisable from time to time for the medical care, education, support, and maintenance in reasonable comfort of the Settlor's wife, taking into consideration to the extent the Trustee deems advisable, any other income or sources of support for the Settlor's wife of which the Trustee knows.

(3) In addition to the income and discretionary payment of principal from this Trust, the Trustee shall pay the Settlor's wife, during her lifetime and upon her written request during the last month of each calendar year of the Trust, an amount from the principal not to exceed during that calendar year the amount of Five Thousand ($5,000) Dollars or Five (5%) percent of the aggregate value of the principal of Trust B on the last day of that calendar year without reduction for the principal payment for that calendar year, whichever is greater. This right of withdrawal is noncumulative, so that if the Settlor's wife does not withdraw, during that calendar year, the full amount to which she is entitled under this paragraph, her right to withdraw the amount not withdrawn shall lapse at the end of that calendar year.

Paragraph (4) of Article VIII in Al's trust would specify the final distribution of Trust B in the same way as Article VII of the joint trust specifies the final distribution of the joint trust estate.

(4) Upon the death of the Settlor's wife, the Trustee shall hold, manage and distribute the Trust Estate for the benefit of Charles C. Smith (born 3/12/70), Darlene D. Smith (born 6/23/75), and Edith E. Smith (born

7/29/76) ("Charles, Darlene, and Edith"). The Trustee shall divide the Trust Estate into equal separate Shares so as to provide One (1) Share for each living beneficiary and One (1) Share for each deceased beneficiary who shall leave issue then living. The Trustee shall hold, manage and distribute each Share provided for a living beneficiary, as set forth in Article IX. The Trustee shall hold, manage, and distribute each Share provided for a deceased beneficiary, as set forth in the Article X.

Article VII and Article VIII in Betty's trust would have Betty's name substituted for Al's and the word "husband" substituted for the word "wife." Lawyers refer to this technique as *reciprocal* documents. Each spouse gives the other the same things.

The trusts in a split estate would also contain two additional articles. One of these is an article which lawyers refer to as a *savings clause* for the transfers from the trust of a deceased spouse to the trust of the surviving spouse. This directs the trustee to select only property which qualifies for the unlimited marital deduction in making these transfers. The following is an example of such an article for Al's trust:

ARTICLE XVIII

Selection of Property for Tax Purposes

The Settlor intends that the gift which he makes to his wife, Betty B. Smith, in Share A of this agreement convey ownership of the property to his wife. The Trustee shall select only those assets for Share A which qualify for the marital deduction under IRC Section 2056. To the greatest extent possible, the Trustee shall select property for Share A which will be ultimately taxable income to a non-charitable beneficiary. The Trustee shall select property which will be ultimately taxable income to a non-charitable beneficiary, to the greatest extent possible, to fund any distributions which qualify as charitable gifts under the Internal Revenue Code. The Trustee shall not construe any other directions under this agreement to conflict with this direction.

The other additional article provides the surviving spouse with one more means of control over Trust B. This article gives him or her the right to change trustees after the death of his or her spouse. This provision can be particularly important in the situation where there is a corporate trustee which the surviving spouse thinks is unresponsive to requests for discretionary payments. "If you don't think I need a new car, I know a corporate trustee who does!"

The following is an example of an article in Al's trust which gives the surviving spouse appropriate leverage over an unresponsive trustee:

ARTICLE XXI

Right of Settlor's Surviving Spouse to Change Trustees

The Settlor's wife may, at any time after the Settlor's death, discharge any Trustee acting under this agreement. If the Settlor's wife wishes to discharge a Trustee, she shall give the Trustee written notice at the Trustee's last-known address. The Settlor's wife shall then appoint a substitute trustee within Thirty (30) days of giving this notice. The Trustee shall deliver the property and records of the Trust Estate and make a full and proper accounting to the substitute trustee within Thirty (30) days after the Settlor's wife has appointed the substitute trustee. When the Trustee has delivered the property and records and made its accounting, it shall be discharged. When the substitute trustee has accepted the property and the accounting, the substitute trustee shall succeed to all the rights, powers, and duties of the Trustee originally named in this agreement.

The sample documents do not include an example of a property ownership agreement, conveyances to the trustees, or declarations of trust. Other than these items, the examples show what a trust and the other estate-planning documents look like.

You will notice that there is a letter which explains that people who have a living trust do not need to make any special provision with respect to their income tax. The IRS refers to a self-directed living trust as a grantor trust. If you are the settlor, trustee, and sole beneficiary, you have complete ownership of the property in your trust. The difference is the management of the property if you become incompetent and when you die.

The last document in the samples is a letter explaining how you transfer property into your living trust. The attorney would give this to Al and Betty *after* they had signed their documents. There is nothing you can do to prepare for having a comprehensive estate plan prepared. Until you sign your trust documents, you can't put anything in your trust. Remember, you can't deed property to an unborn child!

You may ask, "Do I need all of this?" The answer is, "We hope not!" If you can state for certain that you will never become incompetent, you can wait and see and let "the devil take the hindmost." It may be that you are worried about the price. The fees for an estate plan could not come close to the fees you or your family will pay if you don't have one.

JEROME L. HOLLINGSWORTH

Attorney at Law

Licensed in Florida

Michigan & Wisconsin

2500 Tamiami Trail North, Suite 221

Naples, Fl. 33940 *

(813) 263 - 3773

November 30, 1991

Al and Betty Smith
123 Lover's Lane
Naples, FL 33940

Re: Drafts of Estate Planning Documents

Dear Al and Betty:

I am enclosing a preliminary draft of your Living Trust along with a preliminary draft of your Last Will and Testament. I am also enclosing some other documents which I have prepared.

You may want to change Article VII of your trust and Item III of your wills by adding specific instructions with respect to certain items of property. For example, if you wish to give some particular individual a specific parcel of land or some other item which has a record title, you would do this in Article VII of your trust. If you wish to give some individual a particular item of property which has no record title, you would do this in Item III of your will.

Let me now explain these documents to you, beginning with your Living Trust. If you look at the draft documents as you read this letter, I am certain that you will find the documents to be rather simple.

Opening paragraph – This paragraph recites that this is an agreement or contract between Alfred A. Smith and Betty B. Smith as settlors (the persons setting up the trust), Alfred A. Smith and Betty B. Smith as trustees (the persons who manage the trust) and SunBank/Naples, NA as successor trustee.

Article I – This article states that the property in the trust is listed on Schedule A and that the insurance policies payable to the trust or which insure trust property are listed on Schedule B.

Article II – This article states that you may borrow against any life insurance policies which are assigned to the trust.

103

Article III – This article sets up the duties of the trustees during your lifetimes.

Article IV – This article enumerates your rights, as settlors, to make changes in the structure of the trust. It is this article which makes the trust revocable.

Article V – This article permits the successor trustee to pay final expenses after death.

Article VI – This article sets up the succession of trustees. It contains a provision which permits an orderly management of your property in the event the trustee or trustees should become incompetent, without the necessity of a competency hearing in the Probate Court.

Article VII – This article specifies the trustee's duties with respect to management and final distribution of the Trust Estate. You can modify this provision to provide for any plan of distribution you wish, and you can provide for management after your deaths.

Article VIII – This article specifies the trustee's duties during the time when all the children of a deceased beneficiary are under 18 years, and provides for distribution if none of these children reach the age of 18.

Article IX – This article states the trustee duties after the oldest child of a deceased beneficiary reaches the age of 18 years and provides for final distribution of the deceased beneficiary's share.

Article X – This is a spendthrift provision. It precludes any beneficiary under the trust from anticipating income or principal and disposing of this prior to the time payment is due.

Article XI – This article permits an individual or individuals who may be serving as trustee or trustees to appoint a corporate substitute either as sole or joint trustee. An individual would want to do this if there were property to be managed for the benefit of minors.

Article XII – This article permits a successor corporation to assume the duties of a corporate trustee, if there should be one.

Article XIII – This article permits the settlors to change trustees without having to change all of the pronouns referring to the trustee – his, hers, its, etc.

Article XIV – This article specifies the fees for corporate trustee, if there should be one.

Article XV – This article specifies the powers of the trustees with respect to property in the trust.

Article XVI – This article gives a corporate trustee who is presently serving the right to resign.

Article XVII – This article permits you, as settlors of your trust, to change trustees during your lifetimes.

Article XVIII – This article gives the ultimate beneficiaries the power to change trustees after the settlors' deaths.

Article XIX – This article gives a trustee the discretion necessary to manage a trust with beneficiaries such as children or others who are under a legal disability.

Article XX – This article gives a trustee discretion to terminate a trust which may be too small to warrant management.

Article XXI – This article contains a simultaneous death provision. In this case, it states that any beneficiary will be presumed to have predeceased the settlors. This insures that the trust property will be distributed in accordance with the settlors' plan of distribution rather than the plan of distribution of the beneficiary.

Article XXII – This article states that outsiders who deal with a trustee need not inquire as to the powers of the trustee.

Article XXIII – This article specifies the state whose laws will control any interpretation of the trust agreement.

Article XXIV – This article precludes the trust going on perpetually, something which is forbidden by law.

Schedule A – This is where you list the assets which you have placed in the trust. This gives the successor trustee assistance in the event the successor takes over the duties of the trustee. It also reminds you of what is in the trust when you come to dispose of the property for one reason or another.

Schedule B – This is where you list the names of the insurance companies, the policy numbers and the face amounts of any insurance policies which are payable to the trust or which insure trust property.

I shall now explain the various provisions of your will.

Opening Paragraph – This paragraph states the name of the testator or testatrix (person making the will) and revokes all prior wills and codicils (amendments to wills). This paragraph also gives the personal representative the authority to pay the final debts of the testator or testatrix.

Item I – This item nominates the personal representative (person who is to carry out the wishes of the testator or testatrix).

Item II – This item gives the personal representative the authority to pay death taxes.

Item III – This item is used to specifically devise (give away at death) items of personal property. You may want specific things to go to specific persons. You can list these in Item III, and the personal representative will give these things to the designated person prior to dividing up the rest of the personal property not in the trust.

Item IV – This item disposes of the personal property which the testator or testatrix owned at death, other than the personal property which is in the trust.

Item V – This item is a "pourover" provision. It places any property, other than personal property disposed of in Item III or Item IV, into the living trust of the testator or testatrix. The item also contains a provision stating that the scheme of disposition specified in the trust shall control even if the trust is not in effect, for some reason or another, at the time of death.

Item VI – This Item directs the personal representative to seek to have the person or persons of your choosing appointed as legal guardian of any minor children.

Item VII – This item contains a simultaneous death provision. The presumption here is that the devisee survived the testator or testatrix. A person normally wants personal property disposed of in accordance with the distribution scheme of the person receiving it, because this will cause the descent of personal property to continue uninterrupted.

You will also find a Certificate of Trust. You can give a copy of this document to any bank or stock broker who might want to know who the trustee is and what the powers of the trustee are. Additionally, this is the document which we record when you are conveying property out of the trust.

I have provided you with a "Living Will" (Declaration to Physicians). This document directs your family, guardian or any physician who may attend you to terminate treatment if there is no hope of saving you. I have also provided you with a Power of Attorney for Medical Care. This document covers the situation where your are not about to die but are unable to make medical decisions for yourself.

You should also have contingent powers of attorney to cover the event of your being incompetent or unconscious from an accident. In such an event, the successor trustee could not only manage property which you have transferred to the trust, but would be able to transfer property from outside the trust into the trust if you have not done so.

I am enclosing Contingent Durable Powers of Attorney.

I am also enclosing a letter which explains to other people that you do not need to make any special arrangements for income taxes as a result of having a living trust.

You must understand that we can change any portion of these documents very easily while they are in the draft stage. We have stored these documents magnetically and can modify them easily using our computers.

If there is anything concerning these documents which is unclear, do not hesitate to ask me to explain it more fully.

Al and Betty Smith
Drafts of Estate Planning Documents
Page 6

I have dated the documents for December 7, 1991. I look forward to seeing you at 10:00 a.m. on that date. We can make any changes you wish prior to that date or when you come in to execute them.

Very truly yours,

Jerome L. Hollingsworth

JLH/acb

JOINT TRUST AGREEMENT
Alfred and Betty Smith Living Trust

Agreement made December 7, 1991, between Alfred A. Smith and Betty B. Smith (the "Settlors"), Alfred A. Smith and Betty B. Smith (the "Trustees") and SunBank/Naples, NA (the "Successor Trustee"), known as the "Alfred and Betty Smith Living Trust, dated December 7, 1991".

ARTICLE I
Property Transferred to Trustees

The Settlors hereby declare that the Trustees hold title to the real and personal property which now is, and in the future may be, listed on Schedule A, attached to this trust agreement and incorporated into it by reference. Additionally, the Settlors have or will designate the Trustees as the beneficiaries of the insurance policies described in Schedule B, attached to this trust agreement and incorporated into it by reference. This property, and any property which may be titled in the Trustees' names, as Trustees, and the proceeds of any insurance policy of which the Trustees are or may be named the beneficiaries, as invested and reinvested, shall be known as the "Trust Estate". The Trustees shall hold, administer and distribute the Trust Estate as provided for in this agreement.

ARTICLE II
Trustees' Duties Concerning Life Insurance

The rights of the Settlors and the duties of the Trustees with respect to any insurance policies are as follows:

(1) During the Settlors' lifetimes, the Settlors shall have all rights under any life insurance policies payable to the Trustees, including the right to change the beneficiary, to receive any dividends or other earnings of these policies, or cancel these policies outright, without accountability for their actions to the Trustees or any beneficiary under this trust agreement.

(2) The Settlors may assign any policies to any lender, including the Trustees as a lender, as security for any loan to the Settlors or any other person.

(3) The Trustees shall have no responsibility with respect to any policies which they receive in safekeeping except to deliver them upon the Settlors' written request or to hold any policies which the Trustees receive in safekeeping and to deliver them upon the Settlors' written request.

(4) The rights of any assignee of any policy shall be superior to the rights of the Trustees.

(5) Upon the death of the insured under any policy held by or known to and payable to the Trustees, or upon the occurrence of some event prior to the death of the Settlors that matures any insurance policy, the Trustees, in their discretion, either may collect the net proceeds and hold them as part of the principal of the Trust Estate, or may exercise any optional method of settlement available to them.

(6) The Trustees shall deliver any policies on the Settlors' life held by them and payable to any other beneficiaries as those beneficiaries may direct, after the Settlors' death. Payment to, and the receipt of by the Trustees shall be a full discharge of the liability of any insurance company, which need not take notice of this agreement or see to the application of any payment.

(7) The Trustees need not engage in litigation to enforce payment of any policy without indemnification satisfactory to them for any resulting expenses, nor shall the Trustees be responsible for the payment of any premiums on insurance policies unless the Trustees specifically agree, in writing, to be responsible for the payment.

(8) The Trustees shall not be responsible for initiating or perfecting any application for waiver of premium on any insurance policy due to the Settlors' disability.

ARTICLE III
Trustees' Duties During the Settlors' Lifetimes

The Trustees shall hold, manage, invest and reinvest the Trust Estate (if any part of it requires management and investment) and shall collect the income, if any, from the Trust Estate and shall dispose of the net income and principal as follows:

(1) During the Settlors' lifetimes, the Trustees shall pay all the net income from the Trust Estate to the Settlors or apply it to their benefit.

(2) During the Settlors' lifetimes, the Trustees may pay such sums from the principal of the Trust Estate, as in their sole discretion, shall be necessary or advisable from time to time for the Settlors' medical care, comfortable maintenance and welfare, or the Trustees may apply these sums for the Settlors' benefit, taking into consideration to the extent the Trustees deem advisable, any other income or resources of the Settlors of which the Trustees know.

(3) The Trustees shall convey and deliver all or any part of the principal of the Trust Estate to the Settlors, free of trust, upon receipt of a written instrument which the Settlors have signed and which describes the property or the portion of it which the Settlors wish to withdraw.

(4) In the event that both Settlors are either adjudicated to be incompetent or, by reason of illness or mental or physical disability are, in the opinion of two physicians, unable to handle business affairs properly, or in the event that one Settlor is deceased and the other Settlor is either adjudicated to be incompetent or, in the opinion of two physicians, is unable to handle business affairs properly, then the Trustee may, during the Settlors' lifetimes, in addition to the payments of income and principal for the Settlors' benefit, pay to any dependent children of the Settlors, or apply to benefit of any dependent children of the Settlors, such sums from the net income and from the principal of the Trust Estate as in the Trustee's sole discretion shall be necessary or advisable from time to time for the medical care, comfortable maintenance and welfare of any dependent children of the Settlors, taking into consideration to the extent the Trustee deems advisable, any other income or resources of any dependent children of the Settlors of which the Trustee knows.

ARTICLE IV
Settlors' Power to Amend and Revoke

The Settlors may, during their lifetimes: (1) withdraw property from this Trust in any amount and at any time upon giving reasonable notice in writing to the Trustees; (2) add other property to the Trust; (3) change the beneficiaries, their respective shares and the plan of distribution; (4) amend this Trust Agreement in any other respect; (5) revoke this Trust in its entirety or any provision of it; provided, however, the duties or responsibilities of the Trustees shall not be enlarged without the Trustees' consent nor without satisfactory adjustment of the Trustees' compensation.

ARTICLE V
Expenses of Administration

Any person or persons acting as Trustee shall have absolute discretion to pay all or any part of the Settlors' funeral expenses, legally enforceable claims against the Settlors or their estates, reasonable expenses of administration of their estates, any allowances by court order to those dependent upon the Settlors, any estate, inheritance, succession, death or similar taxes payable by reason of the Settlors deaths, together with any interest on or other additions to them, without reimbursement from the Settlors' Personal Representative, from any beneficiary of insurance upon the Settlors' life, or from any other person.

All of these payments, except of interest, shall be charged generally against the principal of the Trust Estate includable in the Settlors' estates for Federal Estate Tax purposes and any interest so paid shall be charged generally against the income of the Settlors' estates. Written statements by the Personal Representative of any sums due and payable by the estate shall be sufficient evidence of their amount and propriety for the protection of the Trustees and the Trustees shall be under no duty to see to the application of any of these payments.

The Trustee shall not use any annuity or payment which the Trustee receives and which is excluded from the Settlors' gross estates under Section 2039 of the Internal Revenue Code to pay any expense, debt, claim or expense of administration. The Trustee shall pay over to the Settlors' Personal Representatives all obligations of the United States Government held under this agreement which may be redeemed at par in payment of federal estate taxes.

ARTICLE VI
Succession of Trustees

The Trustees under this agreement are Alfred A. Smith and Betty B. Smith and the Successor Trustee is SunBank/Naples, NA. Upon the death of the first Trustee, or in the event that either Trustee is either adjudicated to be incompetent or, by reason of illness or mental or physical disability is, in the opinion of two physicians, unable to handle business affairs properly, then the other Trustee shall continue as Trustee. Upon the death of the second Trustee, or in the event that the surviving Trustee or both Trustees are either adjudicated to be incompetent or, by reason of illness or mental or physical disability are, in the opinion of two physicians, unable to handle the duties of Trustees properly, then the Successor Trustee shall assume the duties of the Trustee.

ARTICLE VII
Distribution Upon the Death of the Settlors

Upon the death of the first Settlor to die, the surviving Settlor shall become the sole beneficial owner of the entire Trust Estate, to the same extent and with the same powers as if that Settlor were originally a sole Settlor and had funded the Trust with that Settlor's property, exclusively. Upon the death of both Settlors, the Trustee shall collect any insurance proceeds upon that occasion along with any property which may be added from the Settlors' general estates and shall hold, manage and distribute the Trust Estate for the benefit of Charles C. Smith (born 3/12/70), Darlene D. Smith (born 6/23/75) and Edith E. Smith (born 7/29/76).

The Trustee shall divide the Trust Estate into equal separate Shares so as to provide One (1) Share for each living beneficiary and One (1) Share for each deceased beneficiary who shall leave issue then living. The Trustee shall manage and distribute each Share provided for a living beneficiary, as set forth below. The Trustee shall hold, manage and distribute each Share provided for a deceased beneficiary, as set forth in Article VIII.

(1) Commencing with the date on which each living beneficiary under this agreement attains the age of Eighteen (18) years, the Trustee shall pay to or apply for the benefit of that beneficiary, during his or her lifetime, all of the net income from that beneficiary's Share in convenient installments but no less frequently than quarter-annually.

(2) In addition, the Trustee may pay to or apply for the benefit of that beneficiary such sums from the principal of the Share as in its sole discretion shall be necessary or advisable from time to time for the maintenance, medical care and education of that beneficiary, taking into consideration to the extent the Trustee deems advisable any other income or sources of support for the beneficiary of which the Trustee knows.

(3) When each beneficiary reaches the age of Twenty-five (25) years, the Trustee shall pay One-third (1/3) of that beneficiary's Share to the beneficiary, free of trust.

(4) When each beneficiary reaches the age of Thirty (30) years, the Trustee shall pay the remainder of that beneficiary's Share to the beneficiary, free of trust.

(5) Notwithstanding anything contained in this agreement to the contrary, if any beneficiary under this Article is either adjudicated to be incompetent or, by reason of illness or mental or physical disability is, in the opinion of two physicians, unable to handle his or her own affairs properly, then the Trustee shall not make the distributions of principal specified in paragraphs (3) and (4), above, but shall continue to manage the property as specified in this Article.

(6) If any beneficiary shall not survive to the time of final distribution of that beneficiary's Share and shall die without leaving issue, then the Trustee shall hold, administer and distribute that beneficiary's Share as if that beneficiary had not survived the Settlors.

(7) If any beneficiary shall not survive to the time of final distribution of that beneficiary's Share but shall die leaving issue, the Trustee shall manage that beneficiary's Share for the benefit of the deceased beneficiary's issue, as set forth below.

ARTICLE VIII
Provisions for a Deceased Beneficiary's Children

The Trustee shall hold, administer and distribute each Share provided for the children of the deceased beneficiary as follows:

(1) The Trustee may pay to or apply for the benefit of the deceased beneficiary's children such sums from the principal of the Trust as in its sole discretion shall be necessary or advisable from time to time for their maintenance, medical care and education, taking into consideration to the extent the Trustee deems advisable, any other income or sources of support for the deceased beneficiary's children of which the Trustee knows.

(2) When the oldest living child of the deceased beneficiary attains the age of Eighteen (18) years, the Trustee shall divide the deceased beneficiary's Share into equal and separate Shares so as to provide One (1) Share for each living child of the deceased beneficiary. The Trustee shall hold, administer and distribute these Shares, as set forth below.

(3) If no child of the deceased beneficiary achieves the age of Eighteen (18) years, then the Trustee shall administer the deceased beneficiary's Share in the same manner as if the beneficiary had died without leaving issue.

ARTICLE IX
Final Distribution to a Deceased Beneficiary's Children

After the deceased beneficiary's Share is divided into Shares, the Trustee shall manage each Share as follows:

(1) Commencing with the date on which each child of the deceased beneficiary attains the age of Eighteen (18) years, the Trustee shall pay to or apply for the benefit of that child, during his or her lifetime, all of the net income from that child's Share in convenient installments but no less frequently than quarter-annually.

(2) In addition, the Trustee may pay to or apply for the benefit of each child such sums from the principal of that child's Share as in its sole discretion shall be necessary or advisable from time to time for the maintenance, medical care and education of that child, taking into consideration to the extent the Trustee deems advisable any other income or sources of support for the child of which the Trustee knows.

(3) When each child reaches the age of Twenty-five (25) years, the Trustee shall pay One-third (1/3) of that child's Share to the child, free of trust.

(4) When each child reaches the age of Thirty (30) years, the Trustee shall pay the remainder of that child's Share to the child, free of trust.

(5) Notwithstanding anything contained in this agreement to the contrary, if any beneficiary under this Article is either adjudicated to be incompetent or, by reason of illness or mental or physical disability is, in the opinion of two physicians, unable to handle his or her own affairs properly, then the Trustee shall not make the distributions of principal specified in paragraphs (3) and (4), above, but shall continue to manage the property as specified in this Article.

(6) If any child of the deceased beneficiary shall not survive to the time of final distribution of that child's Share, then the Trustee shall hold, administer and distribute that child's Share as if that child had not survived to the time when the oldest child of the deceased beneficiary reached the age of Eighteen (18) years.

(7) If no child of the deceased beneficiary shall survive to the time of final distribution of that child's Share, then the Trustee shall hold, administer and distribute the deceased child's Share as if the deceased beneficiary had died without leaving issue.

ARTICLE X
Spendthrift Provision

Except as otherwise provided in this agreement, no beneficiary may assign, pledge, sell, transfer or encumber his or her interest, in any manner, nor may any beneficiary anticipate any payments of principal or income payable, or to become payable, to the beneficiary under any trust created under this agreement, nor shall that interest, while in the possession of the Trustee, be liable for or subject to the debts, contracts, obligations, liabilities or torts of any beneficiary.

ARTICLE XI
Right to Appoint Corporate Trustee

Except as otherwise provided in this Trust Agreement, any individual or individuals serving as Trustee or Trustees may, in their sole discretion, appoint a corporate trustee either as sole or joint trustee.

ARTICLE XII
Succession of Corporate Trustees

If any corporate trustee, designated under the terms of this agreement, transfers its trust business to another corporation, for any reason whatsoever, the successor corporation shall assume the position of the designated Trustee without further designation or conveyance.

ARTICLE XIII
Change of Number and Gender of Words Unnecessary

The nouns, verbs, pronouns and pronominal adjectives which refer to the Trustees designated under this agreement are in the singular, plural, masculine, feminine and neuter as appropriate to the Trustees which the Settlors designated originally. There shall be no necessity to change these words in the event the Settlors designate a different Trustee or another Trustee assumes the duties of the designated Trustee under this agreement. However, the terms shall have the same effect as if they had been changed and the proper words substituted.

ARTICLE XIV
Fee for Corporate Trustee

A corporate trustee acting under this agreement shall determine its fee from its Standard Fee Schedule in effect at the time it performs its services. If the corporate trustee does not have a Standard Fee Schedule, then it shall charge a reasonable fee for its services.

ARTICLE XV
Powers of Trustees Under this Agreement

The Trustees' powers with respect to any property, real or personal, at any time held under any provision of this Trust, and without authorization by any court, and in addition to any other rights, powers, authority and privileges granted by any other provision of this Trust or by statute or general rules of law, include the following:

(1) Collect, hold, and retain assets received from the Settlors until, in the judgment of the Trustees, disposition of the assets should be made, and the assets may be retained even though they include an asset in which the Trustees are personally interested.

(2) Receive additions to the assets of the trust which are acceptable to the Trustees.

(3) Continue or participate in the operation of a business or other enterprise, and effect incorporation, dissolution, or, other change in the form of the organization of the business or enterprise. Following the death of the Settlors, the Trustee may continue the business of the Settlors.

(4) Acquire an undivided interest in a trust asset in which the Trustees, in any trust capacity, hold an undivided interest.

(5) Invest and reinvest trust assets in accordance with the provisions of the trust or as provided by law.

(6) Deposit trust funds in any financial institution, including a financial institution operated by the Trustees.

(7) Acquire or dispose of assets, for cash or on credit, at public or private sale; manage, develop, exchange, partition, change the character of, or abandon a trust asset for a term within or extending beyond the term of the trust, in connection with the exercise of any power vested in the Trustees.

(8) Make ordinary or extraordinary repairs or alterations in buildings or other structures, demolish any improvements, or raze existing or erect new party walls or buildings.

(9) Subdivide and develop land, or dedicate land to public use; make or obtain the vacation of plats and adjust boundaries; adjust differences in valuation on exchange or partition by giving or receiving consideration; or dedicate easements to public use without consideration.

(10) Enter for any purpose into a lease as lessor or lessee with or without option to purchase or renew for a term within or extending beyond the term of the trust.

(11) Enter into a lease or arrangement for exploration and removal of minerals or other natural resources or enter into a pooling or unitization agreement.

(12) As to oil, gas, and mineral interests, drill, test, explore, mine, develop, and otherwise exploit the interests; in connection therewith pay from principal or income all delay rentals, lease bonuses, royalties, over-riding royalties, taxes, assessments, and other charges; and surrender or abandon an interest; enter into farmout pooling, unitization, or dryhold contribution agreements in connection therewith; and produce, process, sell, or exchange the production from the interest in a manner and extent as the Trustees, in their sole discretion, deem advisable.

(13) Grant an option involving disposition of a trust asset, or take an option for the acquisition of an asset.

(14) Vote a security, in person or by general or limited proxy.

(15) Pay calls, assessments, and any other sums chargeable or accruing against or on account of securities.

(16) Sell or exercise stock subscription or conversion rights; or consent, directly or through a committee or other agent, to the reorganization, consolidation, merger, dissolution, or liquidation of a corporation or other business enterprise.

(17) Hold land or a security in the name of a nominee or in other form without disclosure of the trust, so that the title to the land or security may pass by delivery, but the Trustees are liable for any act of the nominee in connection with the land or security so held.

(18) Insure the assets of the trust against damage or loss, and the Trustees against liability with respect to third persons.

(19) Borrow money to be repaid from trust assets or otherwise; mortgage or pledge trust assets; and advance money for the protection of the trust, and for expenses, losses, or liabilities sustained in the administration of the trust or because of the holding or ownership of any trust assets, for which advances with any interest the Trustees have a lien on the trust assets as against the beneficiary.

(20) Pay or contest a claim; settle a claim by or against the trust assets by compromise, arbitration, or otherwise; and release, whole or in part, a claim belonging to the trust to the extent that the claim is uncollectable in the opinion of the Trustees.

(21) Pay taxes, assessments, compensation of the Trustees, and other expenses incurred in the collection, care, administration, and production of the trust.

(22) Pay any sum distribution to a beneficiary under legal disability, without liability to the Trustees, by paying the sum to the beneficiary, or by paying the sum for the use of the beneficiary or to a legal representative appointed by the court, or if none to a relative, for the use of the beneficiary.

(23) Effect distribution of property and money in divided or undivided interests or in disproportionate shares or in different kinds of property and adjust resulting differences in valuation.

(24) Employ persons, including attorneys, auditors, investment advisors, discretionary money managers, or agents, even if they are associated with the Trustees, to advise or assist the Trustees in the performance of their administrative duties; act without independent investigation upon their recommendations; and instead of acting personally, employ an agent to perform any act of administration, whether or not discretionary.

(25) Prosecute or defend actions, claims, or proceedings for the protection of trust assets and of the Trustees in the performance of their duties.

(26) Execute and deliver instruments which will accomplish or facilitate the exercise of the powers vested in the Trustees.

(27) Perform, compromise, or refuse performance of the decedents' contracts that continue as obligations of the estate, as they determine under the circumstances. In performing enforceable contracts by the Settlors of the trust to convey or lease land, the Trustee, among other possible choices of action, may do either of the following:

a. Execute and deliver a deed of conveyance for cash payment of all sums remaining due on the purchaser's note for the sum remaining due secured by a mortgage or deed of trust on the land.

b. Deliver a deed in escrow with directions that the proceeds, when paid in accordance with the escrow agreement, be paid to the Trustee, as designated in the escrow agreement.

(28) Satisfy written charitable pledges of the Settlors of the trust irrespective of whether the pledges constitute binding obligations of the Settlors or where properly presented as claims, if in the judgment of the Trustee, the Settlors would have wanted the pledges completed under the circumstances.

(29) Abandon property when, in the opinion of the Trustee, it is valueless, or is so encumbered or in a condition that it is not of benefit to the trust.

(30) Effect a fair and reasonable compromise with a debtor or obligor, or extend, renew, or in any manner modify the terms of an obligation owing to the trust. A Trustee who holds a mortgage, pledge, or other lien upon property of another person, may, in lieu of foreclosure, accept the conveyance or transfer of encumbered assets from the owner thereof in satisfaction of the indebtedness secured by lien.

(31) Provide for exoneration of the Trustees from personal liability in a contract entered into on behalf of the trust.

(32) Sell real property, no matter where it is located, without application to any court.

(33) Invest in long calls and puts or to write covered and naked options and to use option trading as an investment vehicle and to trade on margin as related to option or any other securities trading.

(34) Invest in certificates of deposit or other savings instruments of like character issued by any financial institution including a bank operated by the Trustees.

(35) Sell, mortgage, pledge, hypothecate, exchange, invest, reinvest and otherwise manage all or any part of the Trust property in investments including, but not limited to stocks, bonds, convertible securities, annuities, insurance contracts, options, mutual funds, limited partnerships, real estate, commingled funds or common trust funds and deposits managed by any financial institution.

(36) In the general administration of a trust, a Trustee shall exercise reasonable judgment and discretion for what the Trustee believes to be in the best interest of the trust and the persons designated to benefit from the trust. A Trustee's powers include the following:

a. Exclusion from or inclusion in the gross estate of any asset, in the first instance, for Federal Estate Tax purpose.

b. Valuation of an asset, in the first instance, for Federal Estate Tax purposes.

c. Election of date of death or alternate valuation for Federal Estate Tax purposes.

d. Joining with the surviving spouse or his or her Personal Representative, in the execution and filing of any joint income tax return and consenting to any gift tax return filed by the spouse, or his or her Personal Representative.

e. Election to claim expenses or losses as either income or estate tax deductions, and shall not make an adjustment between income and principal of the estate because of this election.

(37) In the exercise of its powers including the powers granted by this article and where the applicable provisions of the Internal Revenue Code confer a benefit or impose a detriment upon a trust or estate or persons designated to benefit from a trust or estate, the Trustee or Personal Representative shall not restore an interest to the position otherwise contemplated by the person having authority to act in respect to that interest through adjustment between income and principal.

(38) The Trustee shall not be accountable or responsible to any person interested in the probate estates of the Settlors, and a Personal Representative shall not be accountable or responsible to any person interested in the trust, for the manner in which each exercises any discretion or authority or election afforded under this article.

(39) A Trustee shall not use funds from sources which are exempt for Federal Estate Tax purposes for payment of taxes, claims, and administrative expenses of decedents' estates or trusts.

ARTICLE XVI
Right of Corporate Trustee to Resign

Any corporate trustee may resign its trusteeship under this agreement at any time. If a corporate trustee wishes to resign during the Settlors' lifetimes or the lifetime of either of them, it shall give the Settlors or surviving Settlor written notice at the Settlor's last known address. The Settlors or the surviving Settlor shall appoint a substitute trustee within Thirty (30) days of receiving notice. In the event the Settlors or Settlor does not appoint a substitute trustee within Thirty (30) days or after the Settlor's death, the corporate trustee may apply to a court of competent jurisdiction to have the court appoint a substitute trustee. The corporate trustee shall deliver the property and records of the Trust Estate and make a full and proper accounting to the substitute trustee within Thirty (30) days after the Settlors or Settlor or the court has appointed the substitute trustee. When the corporate trustee has delivered the property and records and made its accounting, it shall be discharged. When the substitute trustee has accepted the property and the accounting, the substitute trustee shall succeed to all the rights, powers and duties of the Trustee originally named in this agreement.

ARTICLE XVII
Right of Settlors to Change Trustees

The Settlors may, at any time during their lifetimes or the lifetime of either of them, discharge any Trustee named or acting under this agreement. The Settlors or surviving Settlor wishing to discharge a Trustee, shall give the Trustee written notice at the Trustee's last known address. The Settlors or the surviving Settlor shall then appoint a substitute trustee within Thirty (30) days of giving this notice. If the Trustee which has been discharged is currently acting as Trustee, the Trustee shall deliver the property and records of the Trust Estate and make a full and proper accounting to the substitute trustee within Thirty (30) days after the Settlors or surviving Settlor have appointed the substitute trustee. When the Trustee has delivered the property and records and made its accounting, it shall be discharged. When the substitute trustee has accepted the property and the accounting, the substitute trustee shall succeed to all the rights, powers and duties of the Trustee originally named in this agreement.

ARTICLE XVIII
Right of Residual Beneficiaries to Change Trustees

At any time after the death of both Settlors, the residual beneficiaries with a present interest in the income from the Trust Estate or with a right to receive the principal of the Trust Estate may discharge any Trustee acting under this agreement by a majority vote, with the number of votes for each beneficiary proportionate to the beneficiary's present interest in the Trust Estate. In the event any of these beneficiaries are under the age of majority, their conservator, custodial parent or guardian, in that order of preference, shall be entitled to vote their interests. If the residual beneficiaries wish to discharge a Trustee, they shall give the Trustee written notice at the Trustee's last known address, naming the new substitute corporate trustee. The Trustee shall deliver the property and records of the Trust Estate and make a full and proper accounting to the substitute corporate trustee within Thirty (30) days after receiving notice of the change of trustees. When the Trustee has delivered the property and records and made its accounting, it shall be discharged. When the substitute corporate trustee has accepted the property and the accounting, the substitute corporate trustee shall succeed to all the rights, powers and duties of the Trustee originally named.

ARTICLE XIX
Management for Legally Incompetent Persons

In case the income or principal payment under any trust created under this trust agreement or any share of it shall become payable to a person under the age of Twenty-one (21), or to a person under legal disability, or to a person not adjudicated incompetent, but who, by reason of illness or mental or physical disability, is, in the opinion of the Trustee unable to administer these amounts properly, then the Trustee may pay these amounts in any of the following ways, as the Trustee deems best: (1) directly to the beneficiary; (2) to the legally appointed guardian of the beneficiary; (3) to some relative or friend for the care, support and education of the beneficiary; (4) directly to third persons for the beneficiary's care, support and education.

ARTICLE XX
Right to Terminate Small Trust

If the Trustee, at any time, in its absolute discretion, determines that it is uneconomical to continue any trust created under this agreement because of its size, the Trustee may terminate the trust and distribute the trust property to another trust for the benefit of the same person or persons, to the person or persons then entitled to receive or have the benefit of the income from it or to the legal representative of these persons. If there is more than one income beneficiary, the Trustee shall make distribution to the income beneficiaries in the proportion in which they are beneficiaries or if no proportion is designated, then in equal shares to the beneficiaries.

ARTICLE XXI
Simultaneous Death Provision

If any beneficiary and the Settlor or the Settlors should die under circumstances as would render it doubtful whether the beneficiary or the Settlor or the Settlors died first, then it shall be conclusively presumed for the purposes of the Trust that the beneficiary predeceased the Settlor or the Settlors.

ARTICLE XXII
Third Persons Dealing with a Trustee

Third persons dealing with a Trustee acting under this agreement or assisting a Trustee in the conduct of a transaction may assume, without inquiry, that the Trustee has the power to carry out the transaction and is exercising the power properly. Third persons are not bound to inquire whether the Trustee may act or is exercising the power properly. Third persons, without actual knowledge that the Trustee is exceeding his powers or exercising them improperly, are protected fully in dealing with the Trustee as if the Trustee possessed and properly exercised the powers he purports to exercise. Third persons need not see to the proper application of property paid or delivered to the Trustee.

ARTICLE XXIII
State Law to Govern

This Trust Agreement and the trusts created by it shall be constructed under the laws of the State of Florida, the situs of the trust.

ARTICLE XXIV
Perpetuities Savings Clause

Notwithstanding anything in this agreement to the contrary, the trusts created under it shall terminate not later than Twenty-one (21) years after the death of the last survivor of the Settlors and their issue living on the date of the death of the second Settlor to die, when the Trustee shall distribute each remaining trust to the beneficiary or beneficiaries of the current income from it, and if there is more than one beneficiary, in the proportion in which they are beneficiaries or, if the trust agreement does not designate a proportion, then in equal shares to the beneficiaries.

In Witness Whereof, the parties have set their hands.

Jerome L. Hollingsworth	Alfred A. Smith, Settlor
Angie C. Badenski	Betty B. Smith, Settlor
	Alfred A. Smith, Trustee
	Betty B. Smith, Trustee

SunBank/Naples, N.A.
Successor Trustee

By:_____
Donald H. Kolb
Executive Vice President

STATE OF FLORIDA ss
COLLIER COUNTY

On December 7, 1991, Alfred A. Smith and Betty B. Smith produced their driver's licenses as identification and acknowledged this instrument, declaring it to be made of their free will and deed.

Angie C. Badenski, Notary Public
State of Florida at Large
Commission No. AA 753552
My commission expires 2/26/94

(NOTARY SEAL)

This Instrument Prepared By:
Jerome L. Hollingsworth
Attorney at Law
Post Office Box 8124
Naples, FL 33941 - 8124
(813) 263-3773

JOINT TRUST AGREEMENT
Alfred and Betty Smith Living Trust

Schedule A

JOINT TRUST AGREEMENT
Alfred and Betty Smith Living Trust

Schedule B

LAST WILL AND TESTAMENT
of
Alfred A. Smith

I, Alfred A. Smith, a resident of and domiciled in Naples, Collier County, Florida, make, publish and declare this to be my Last Will and Testament, revoking all Wills and Codicils which I have made previously.

I declare that all my legally enforceable debts, secured and unsecured, be paid as soon as practicable after my death.

ITEM I

I nominate and appoint Betty B. Smith as Personal Representative of my estate and direct that she shall serve without bond. If for any reason Betty B. Smith is unable or unwilling to serve, or to continue to serve, then I nominate and appoint Charles C. Smith as substitute or successor Personal Representative and direct that he shall serve without bond. If for any reason Charles C. Smith is unable or unwilling to serve, or to continue to serve, then I nominate and appoint SunBank/Naples, NA as substitute or successor Personal Representative and direct that it shall serve without bond.

ITEM II

I direct my Personal Representative to pay all estate, inheritance, succession, death or similar taxes (except generation-skipping transfer taxes) assessed against my probate estate out of my residuary estate and shall not charge any recipient, beneficiary, transferee or owner of any property or interests in property included in my probate estate.

ITEM III

My tangible personal property shall be distributed in accordance with the provisions of ITEM IV of this, my Last Will and Testament. However, I may leave a written statement or list disposing of certain items of my tangible personal property. Any such statement or list in existence at the time of my death shall be determinative with respect to all items devised by it. If my personal representative does not file a written statement or list and properly identifies it within thirty days after the personal representative qualifies, it shall be presumed that there is no such statement or list and my personal representative shall ignore any subsequently discovered statement or list.

ITEM IV

I give to my wife, Betty B. Smith, if she survives me, all of my tangible personal property, whatsoever, including, but not limited to all household and office effects and goods, household furniture, automobiles, works of art, jewelry, silverware, books, clothing, and all other personal effects. In making this gift, I do not wish to indicate that I claim ownership of any tangible personal property which my wife may own already.

If my wife does not survive me, then I direct that my Personal Representative divide all of this property, as equally as possible, among those of my children, Charles C. Smith (born 3/12/70), Darlene D. Smith (born 6/23/75) and Edith E. Smith (born 7/29/76), who survive me, having due regard for their personal preference. If none of these children survive me, then all of this property shall become part of the residue of my estate. There shall be no adjustment in the event any of my children receives, under this provision, property of a greater value than that received by another.

ITEM V

I give all the rest, residue and remainder of my property of every kind and description (including lapsed legacies and devises), wherever situate and whether acquired before or after the execution of this Will, to Betty B. Smith as Trustee of the Alfred and Betty Smith Living Trust dated December 7, 1991, executed prior to the execution of this will. If Betty B. Smith shall not survive me, then I give all the rest, residue and remainder of my property of every kind and description (including lapsed legacies and devises), wherever situate and whether acquired before or after the execution of this Will, to SunBank/Naples, NA as Successor Trustee under that same Trust Agreement. The Trustee or the Successor Trustee shall add the property devised by this Item to the corpus of the Trust and shall hold, administer and distribute that property in accordance with the provisions of the Trust Agreement, including any amendments to the trust which were made before my death.

If for any reason that Trust is not in force at the time of my death, or if this gift to the Trustee of that Trust is held invalid, then I direct that this gift shall be held and managed in exactly the manner described in the instrument of trust now in existence and by the same Trustee, and for that purpose only, I hereby incorporate that instrument of Trust, as it now stands, by reference into this, my Last Will and Testament.

ITEM VI

If my wife, Betty B. Smith, is no longer living at the time of my death, and any of my children have not yet reached the age of 18, I direct my Personal Representative to institute proceedings to have a guardian or guardians appointed for the minor child or children in accordance with my wishes as expressed most recently prior to my death in a letter which shall be in the possession of the Trustee of the Living Trust specified in Item V of this, my Last Will and Testament.

ITEM VII

If any beneficiary under this Last Will and Testament and I should die under circumstances as would render it doubtful whether the beneficiary or I died first, then it shall be conclusively presumed for the purposes of this, my Last Will and Testament, that the beneficiary survived me.

In Witness Whereof, I have set my hand on December 7, 1991.

_____
Alfred A. Smith

The foregoing Will, consisting of three typewritten pages, this included, the first two pages of which bear the signature of the Testator on the margin, was signed, published and declared on December 7, 1991, by the Testator as and for his Last Will and Testament in our presence, and we, at his request and in his presence, and in the presence of each other, have subscribed our names as witnesses on the date above.

_____ of Naples, Florida
Jerome L. Hollingsworth

_____ of Naples, Florida
Elizabeth S. Hollingsworth

PROOF OF LAST WILL AND TESTAMENT

We, Alfred A. Smith, Jerome L. Hollingsworth and Elizabeth S. Hollingsworth, the Testator and the witnesses, respectively, whose names are signed to the foregoing instrument, having been sworn, declared to the undersigned officer that the Testator, in the presence of witnesses, signed the instrument as his Last Will and Testament, that the Testator signed for himself and that each of the witnesses, in the presence of the Testator and in the presence of each other, signed the Will as a witness.

_____
Alfred A. Smith

_____
Jerome L. Hollingsworth

_____
Elizabeth S. Hollingsworth

STATE OF FLORIDA
COLLIER COUNTY　　ss

Subscribed and sworn to before me on December 7, 1991, by Alfred A. Smith, the Testator, who produced his driver's license as identification, and by Jerome L. Hollingsworth and Elizabeth S. Hollingsworth, the witnesses.

_____

(NOTARY SEAL)

Angie C. Badenski, Notary Public
State of Florida at Large
Commission No. AA 753552
My commission expires 2/26/94

This Instrument Prepared By:
Jerome L. Hollingsworth
Attorney at Law
Post Office Box 8124
Naples, FL 33941 – 8124
(813) 263–3773

LAST WILL AND TESTAMENT
of
Betty B. Smith

I, Betty B. Smith, a resident of and domiciled in Naples, Collier County, Florida, make, publish and declare this to be my Last Will and Testament, revoking all Wills and Codicils which I have made previously.

I declare that all my legally enforceable debts, secured and unsecured, be paid as soon as practicable after my death.

ITEM I

I nominate and appoint Alfred A. Smith as Personal Representative of my estate and direct that he shall serve without bond. If for any reason Alfred A. Smith is unable or unwilling to serve, or to continue to serve, then I nominate and appoint Charles C. Smith as substitute or successor Personal Representative and direct that he shall serve without bond. If for any reason Charles C. Smith is unable or unwilling to serve, or to continue to serve, then I nominate and appoint SunBank/Naples, NA as substitute or successor Personal Representative and direct that it shall serve without bond.

ITEM II

I direct my Personal Representative to pay all estate, inheritance, succession, death or similar taxes (except generation-skipping transfer taxes) assessed against my probate estate out of my residuary estate and shall not charge any recipient, beneficiary, transferee or owner of any property or interests in property included in my probate estate.

ITEM III

My tangible personal property shall be distributed in accordance with the provisions of ITEM IV of this, my Last Will and Testament. However, I may leave a written statement or list disposing of certain items of my tangible personal property. Any such statement or list in existence at the time of my death shall be determinative with respect to all items devised by it. If my personal representative does not file a written statement or list and properly identifies it within thirty days after the personal representative qualifies, it shall be presumed that there is no such statement or list and my personal representative shall ignore any subsequently discovered statement or list.

ITEM IV

I give to my husband, Alfred A. Smith, if he survives me, all of my tangible personal property, whatsoever, including, but not limited to all household and office effects and goods, household furniture, automobiles, works of art, jewelry, silverware, books, clothing, and all other personal effects. In making this gift, I do not wish to indicate that I claim ownership of any tangible personal property which my husband may own already.

If my husband does not survive me, then I direct that my Personal Representative divide all of this property, as equally as possible, among those of my children, Charles C. Smith (born 3/12/70), Darlene D. Smith (born 6/23/75) and Edith E. Smith (born 7/29/76), who survive me, having due regard for their personal preference. If none of these children survive me, then all of this property shall become part of the residue of my estate. There shall be no adjustment in the event any of my children receives, under this provision, property of a greater value than that received by another.

ITEM V

I give all the rest, residue and remainder of my property of every kind and description (including lapsed legacies and devises), wherever situate and whether acquired before or after the execution of this Will, to Alfred A. Smith as Trustee of the Alfred and Betty Smith Living Trust dated December 7, 1991, executed prior to the execution of this will. If Alfred A. Smith shall not survive me, then I give all the rest, residue and remainder of my property of every kind and description (including lapsed legacies and devises), wherever situate and whether acquired before or after the execution of this Will, to SunBank/Naples, NA as Successor Trustee under that same Trust Agreement. The Trustee or the Successor Trustee shall add the property devised by this Item to the corpus of the Trust and shall hold, administer and distribute that property in accordance with the provisions of the Trust Agreement, including any amendments to the trust which were made before my death.

If for any reason that Trust is not in force at the time of my death, or if this gift to the Trustee of that Trust is held invalid, then I direct that this gift shall be held and managed in exactly the manner described in the instrument of trust now in existence and by the same Trustee, and for that purpose only, I hereby incorporate that instrument of Trust, as it now stands, by reference into this, my Last Will and Testament.

ITEM VI

If my husband, Alfred A. Smith, is no longer living at the time of my death, and any of my children have not yet reached the age of 18, I direct my Personal Representative to institute proceedings to have a guardian or guardians appointed for the minor child or children in accordance with my wishes as expressed most recently prior to my death in a letter which shall be in the possession of the Trustee of the Living Trust specified in Item V of this, my Last Will and Testament.

ITEM VII

If any beneficiary under this Last Will and Testament and I should die under circumstances as would render it doubtful whether the beneficiary or I died first, then it shall be conclusively presumed for the purposes of this, my Last Will and Testament, that the beneficiary survived me.

In Witness Whereof, I have set my hand on December 7, 1991.

_____
                                Betty B. Smith

The foregoing Will, consisting of three typewritten pages, this included, the first two pages of which bear the signature of the Testatrix on the margin, was signed, published and declared on December 7, 1991, by the Testatrix as and for her Last Will and Testament in our presence, and we, at her request and in her presence, and in the presence of each other, have subscribed our names as witnesses on the date above.

_____ of Naples, Florida
Jerome L. Hollingsworth

_____ of Naples, Florida
Elizabeth S. Hollingsworth

PROOF OF LAST WILL AND TESTAMENT

We, Betty B. Smith, Jerome L. Hollingsworth and Elizabeth S. Hollingsworth, the Testatrix and the witnesses, respectively, whose names are signed to the foregoing instrument, having been sworn, declared to the undersigned officer that the Testatrix, in the presence of witnesses, signed the instrument as her Last Will and Testament, that the Testatrix signed for herself and that each of the witnesses, in the presence of the Testatrix and in the presence of each other, signed the Will as a witness.

_____
Betty B. Smith

_____
Jerome L. Hollingsworth

_____
Elizabeth S. Hollingsworth

STATE OF FLORIDA
COLLIER COUNTY   ss

Subscribed and sworn to before me on December 7, 1991, by Betty B. Smith, the Testatrix, who produced her driver's license as identification, and by Jerome L. Hollingsworth and Elizabeth S. Hollingsworth, the witnesses.

_____
Angie C. Badenski, Notary Public
State of Florida at Large
Commission No. AA 753552
My commission expires 2/26/94

(NOTARY SEAL)

This Instrument Prepared By:
Jerome L. Hollingsworth
Attorney at Law
Post Office Box 8124
Naples, FL 33941 – 8124
(813) 263-3773

CERTIFICATE OF TRUST EXISTENCE AND AUTHORITY

To Whom it May Concern:

Alfred A. Smith and Betty B. Smith established a trust on December 7, 1991, which is known as the "Alfred and Betty Smith Living Trust, dated December 7, 1991".

This is a revocable living trust under its terms.

ARTICLE IV
Settlors' Power to Amend and Revoke

The Settlors may, during their lifetimes: (1) withdraw property from this Trust in any amount and at any time upon giving reasonable notice in writing to the Trustees; (2) add other property to the Trust; (3) change the beneficiaries, their respective shares and the plan of distribution; (4) amend this Trust Agreement in any other respect; (5) revoke this Trust in its entirety or any provision of it; provided, however, the duties or responsibilities of the Trustees shall not be enlarged without the Trustees' consent nor without satisfactory adjustment of the Trustees' compensation.

The succession of trustees is as specified below:

ARTICLE VI
Succession of Trustees

The Trustees under this agreement are Alfred A. Smith and Betty B. Smith and the Successor Trustee is SunBank/Naples, NA. Upon the death of the first Trustee, or in the event that either Trustee is either adjudicated to be incompetent or, by reason of illness or mental or physical disability is, in the opinion of two physicians, unable to handle their own affairs properly, then the other Trustee shall continue as Trustee. Upon the death of the second Trustee, or in the event that both Trustees are either adjudicated to be incompetent or, by reason of illness or mental or physical disability are, in the opinion of two physicians, unable to handle their duties as Trustees properly, then the Successor Trustee shall assume the duties of the Trustee.

Under the terms of the Trust Agreement, any Trustee who is currently acting has the power to do the following:

ARTICLE XIII
Change of Number and Gender of Words Unnecessary

The nouns, verbs, pronouns and pronominal adjectives which refer to the Trustees designated under this agreement are in the singular, plural, masculine, feminine and neuter as appropriate to the Trustees which the Settlors designated originally. There shall be no necessity to change these words in the event the Settlors designate a different Trustee or another Trustee assumes the duties of the designated Trustee under this agreement. However, the terms shall have the same effect as if they had been changed and the proper words substituted.

ARTICLE XV
Powers of Trustees Under the Trust Agreement

The Trustees' powers with respect to any property, real or personal, at any time held under any provision of this Trust, and without authorization by any court, and in addition to any other rights, powers, authority and privileges granted by any other provision of this Trust or by statute or general rules of law, include the following:

(1) Collect, hold, and retain assets received from the Settlors until, in the judgment of the Trustees, disposition of the assets should be made, and the assets may be retained even though they include an asset in which the Trustees are personally interested.

(2) Receive additions to the assets of the trust which are acceptable to the Trustees.

(3) Continue or participate in the operation of a business or other enterprise, and effect incorporation, dissolution, or other change in the form of the organization of the business or enterprise. Following the death of the Settlors, the Trustee may continue the business of the Settlors.

(4) Acquire an undivided interest in a trust asset in which the Trustees, in any trust capacity, hold an undivided interest.

(5) Invest and reinvest trust assets in accordance with the provisions of the trust or as provided by law.

(6) Deposit trust funds in any financial institution, including a financial institution operated by the Trustees.

(7) Acquire or dispose of assets, for cash or on credit, at public or private sale; manage, develop, exchange, partition, change the character of, or abandon a trust asset for a term within or extending beyond the term of the trust, in connection with the exercise of any power vested in the Trustees.

(8) Make ordinary or extraordinary repairs or alterations in buildings or other structures, demolish any improvements, or raze existing or erect new party walls or buildings.

(9) Subdivide and develop land, or dedicate land to public use; make or obtain the vacation of plats and adjust boundaries; adjust differences in valuation on exchange or partition by giving or receiving consideration; or dedicate easements to public use without consideration.

(10) Enter for any purpose into a lease as lessor or lessee with or without option to purchase or renew for a term within or extending beyond the term of the trust.

(11) Enter into a lease or arrangement for exploration and removal of minerals or other natural resources or enter into a pooling or unitization agreement.

(12) As to oil, gas, and mineral interests, drill, test, explore, mine, develop, and otherwise exploit the interests; in connection therewith pay from principal or income all delay rentals, lease bonuses, royalties, overriding royalties, taxes, assessments, and other charges; and surrender or abandon an interest; enter into farmout pooling, unitization, or dryhold contribution agreements in connection therewith; and produce, process, sell, or exchange the production from the interest in a manner and extent as the Trustees, in their sole discretion, deem advisable.

(13) Grant an option involving disposition of a trust asset, or take an option for the acquisition of an asset.

(14) Vote a security, in person or by general or limited proxy.

(15) Pay calls, assessments, and any other sums chargeable or accruing against or on account of securities.

(16) Sell or exercise stock subscription or conversion rights; or consent, directly or through a committee or other agent, to the reorganization, consolidation, merger, dissolution, or liquidation of a corporation or other business enterprise.

(17) Hold land or a security in the name of a nominee or in other form without disclosure of the trust, so that the title to the land or security may pass by delivery, but the Trustees are liable for any act of the nominee in connection with the land or security so held.

(18) Insure the assets of the trust against damage or loss, and the Trustees against liability with respect to third persons.

(19) Borrow money to be repaid from trust assets or otherwise; mortgage or pledge trust assets; and advance money for the protection of the trust, and for expenses, losses, or liabilities sustained in the administration of the trust or because of the holding or ownership of any trust assets, for which advances with any interest the Trustees have a lien on the trust assets as against the beneficiary.

(20) Pay or contest a claim; settle a claim by or against the trust assets by compromise, arbitration, or otherwise; and release, whole or in part, a claim belonging to the trust to the extent that the claim is uncollectable in the opinion of the Trustees.

(21) Pay taxes, assessments, compensation of the Trustees, and other expenses incurred in the collection, care, administration, and production of the trust.

(22) Pay any sum distribution to a beneficiary under legal disability, without liability to the Trustees, by paying the sum to the beneficiary, or by paying the sum for the use of the beneficiary or to a legal representative appointed by the court, or if none to a relative, for the use of the beneficiary.

(23) Effect distribution of property and money in divided or undivided interests or in disproportionate share or in different kinds of property and adjust resulting differences in valuation.

(24) Employ persons, including attorneys, auditors, investment advisors, discretionary money managers, or agents, even if they are associated with the Trustees, to advise or assist the trustee in the performance of their administrative duties; act without independent investigation upon their recommendations; and instead of acting personally, employ an agent to perform any act of administration, whether or not discretionary.

(25) Prosecute or defend actions, claims, or proceedings for the protection of trust assets and of the Trustees in the performance of their duties.

(26) Execute and deliver instruments which will accomplish or facilitate the exercise of the powers vested in the Trustees.

(27) Perform, compromise, or refuse performance of the decedents' contracts that continue as obligations of the estate, as they determine under the circumstances. In performing enforceable contracts by the Settlors of the trust to convey or lease land, the Trustee, among other possible choices of action, may do either of the following:

a. Execute and deliver a deed of conveyance for cash payment of all sums remaining due on the purchaser's note for the sum remaining due secured by a mortgage or deed of trust on the land.

b. Deliver a deed in escrow with directions that the proceeds, when paid in accordance with the escrow agreement, be paid to the Trustee, as designated in the escrow agreement.

(28) Satisfy written charitable pledges of the Settlors of the trust irrespective of whether the pledges constitute binding obligations of the Settlors or where properly presented as claims, if in the judgment of the Trustee, the Settlors would have wanted the pledges completed under the circumstances.

(29) Abandon property when, in the opinion of the Trustee, it is valueless, or is so encumbered or in a condition that it is not of benefit to the trust.

(30) Effect a fair and reasonable compromise with a debtor or obligor, or extend, renew, or in any manner modify the terms of an obligation owing to the trust. A Trustee who holds a mortgage, pledge, or other lien upon property of another person, may, in lieu of foreclosure, accept the conveyance or transfer of encumbered assets from the owner thereof in satisfaction of the indebtedness secured by lien.

(31) Provide for exoneration of the Trustees from personal liability in a contract entered into on behalf of the trust.

(32) Sell real property, no matter where it is located, without application to any court.

(33) Invest in long calls and puts or to write covered and naked options and to use option trading as an investment vehicle and to trade on margin as related to option or any other securities trading.

(34) Invest in certificates of deposit or other savings instruments of like character issued by any financial institution, including a financial institution operated by the Trustees.

(35) Sell, mortgage, pledge, hypothecate, exchange, invest, reinvest and otherwise manage all or any part of the Trust property in investments including, but not limited to stocks, bonds, convertible securities, annuities, insurance contracts, options, mutual funds, limited partnerships, real estate, commingled funds or common trust funds and deposits managed by any financial institution.

(36) In the general administration of a trust, a Trustee shall exercise reasonable judgment and discretion for what the Trustee believes to be the best interest of the trust and the persons designated to benefit from the trust. A Trustee's powers include the following:

a. Exclusion from or inclusion in the gross estate of any asset, in the first instance, for Federal Estate Tax purpose.

b. Valuation of an asset, in the first instance, for Federal Estate Tax purposes.

c. Election of date of death or alternate valuation for Federal Estate Tax purposes.

d. Joining with the surviving spouse or his or her Personal Representative, in the execution and filing of any joint income tax return and consenting to any gift tax return filed by the spouse, or his or her Personal Representative.

e. Election to claim expenses or losses as either income or estate tax deductions, and shall not make an adjustment between income and principal of the estate because of this election.

(37) In the exercise of its powers, including the powers granted by this article, and where the applicable provisions of the Internal Revenue Code confer a benefit or impose a detriment upon a trust or estate or persons designated to benefit from a trust or estate, the Trustee or Personal Representative shall not restore an interest to the position otherwise contemplated by the person having authority to act in respect to that interest through adjustment between income and principal.

(38) The Trustee shall not be accountable or responsible to any person interested in the probate estates of the Settlors, and a Personal Representative shall not be accountable or responsible to any person interested in the trust, for the manner in which each exercises any discretion or authority or election afforded under this article.

(39) A Trustee shall not use funds from sources which are exempt for Federal Estate Tax purposes for payment of taxes, claims, and administrative expenses of decedents' estates or trusts.

ARTICLE XXII
Third Persons Dealing with a Trustee

Third persons dealing with a Trustee acting under this agreement or assisting a Trustee in the conduct of a transaction may assume, without inquiry, that the Trustee has the power to carry out the transaction and is exercising the power properly. Third persons are not bound to inquire whether the Trustee may act or is exercising the power properly. Third persons, without actual knowledge that the Trustee is exceeding his powers or exercising them improperly, are protected fully in dealing with the Trustee as if the Trustee possessed and properly exercised the powers he purports to exercise. Third persons need not see to the proper application of property paid or delivered to the Trustee.

A photostatic copy of this Certificate of Trust Existence and Authority shall serve equally as well and have the same legal significance as the original.

In Witness Whereof, the parties have set their hands.

_____   _____
Jerome L. Hollingsworth   Alfred A. Smith, Settlor

_____   _____
Angie C. Badenski   Betty B. Smith, Settlor

                                   _____
                                   Alfred A. Smith, Trustee

                                   _____
                                   Betty B. Smith, Trustee

SunBank/Naples, N.A.
Successor Trustee

By:_____
                                   Donald H. Kolb
                            Executive Vice President

STATE OF FLORIDA   ss
COLLIER COUNTY

On December 7, 1991, Alfred A. Smith and Betty B. Smith produced their driver's licenses as identification and acknowledged this instrument, declaring it to be made of their free will and deed.

                           _____
(NOTARY SEAL)   Angie C. Badenski, Notary Public
                             State of Florida at Large
                            Commission No. AA 753552
                           My commission expires 2/26/94

This Instrument Prepared By:
Jerome L. Hollingsworth
Attorney at Law
Post Office Box 8124
Naples, FL 33941 - 8124
(813) 263-3773

DECLARATION TO PHYSICIANS

Declaration made December 7, 1991.

I, Alfred A. Smith, being of sound mind, willfully and voluntarily state my desire that my dying may not be artificially prolonged under the circumstances set forth below:

1. If I have an incurable injury or illness certified to be a terminal condition by two physicians who have personally examined me, one of whom is my attending physician, and if the physicians have determined that there can be no recovery whether or not life-sustaining procedures are utilized because the application of life-sustaining procedures would serve only to prolong artificially the dying process, I direct that life-sustaining procedures be withheld or withdrawn and that I be permitted to die naturally, with only the administration of medical procedures deemed necessary to alleviate pain. I further direct that nutrition and hydration be withheld or withdrawn when the application of such procedures would serve only to prolong artificially the process of dying.

2. If I am unable to give direction regarding the use of life-sustaining procedures, I intend that my family and physician honor this declaration as the final expression of my legal right to refuse medical or surgical treatment and to accept the consequences of this refusal.

I understand this declaration and I am emotionally and mentally competent to make this declaration.

_____
Alfred A. Smith

I know the declarant personally and I believe him to be of sound mind. I am not related to the declarant by blood or marriage, and am not entitled to any portion of the declarant's estate under any will of the declarant. I am neither the declarant's attending physician nor an employee of the attending physician or of the inpatient health care facility in which the declarant may be a patient and I have no claim against the declarant's estate at this time.

_____
Jerome L. Hollingsworth

_____
Elizabeth S. Hollingsworth

PROOF OF DECLARATION

We, Alfred A. Smith, Jerome L. Hollingsworth and Elizabeth S. Hollingsworth, the declarant and the witnesses, respectively, whose names are signed to the foregoing instrument, having been sworn, declared to the undersigned officer that the declarant, in the presence of witnesses, signed the instrument as his intended declaration, that the declarant signed for himself and that each of the witnesses, in the presence of the declarant and in the presence of each other, signed as a witness.

_____
Alfred A. Smith

_____
Jerome L. Hollingsworth

_____
Elizabeth S. Hollingsworth

STATE OF FLORIDA
COLLIER COUNTY   ss

Subscribed and sworn to before me on December 7, 1991, by Alfred A. Smith, the declarant, who produced his driver's license as identification, and by Jerome L. Hollingsworth and Elizabeth S. Hollingsworth, the witnesses.

_____
(NOTARY SEAL)   Angie C. Badenski, Notary Public
State of Florida at Large
Commission No. AA 753552
My commission expires 2/26/94

This Instrument Prepared By:
Jerome L. Hollingsworth
Attorney at Law
Post Office Box 8124
Naples, FL 33941 – 8124
(813) 263–3773

144

DECLARATION TO PHYSICIANS

Declaration made December 7, 1991.

I, Betty B. Smith, being of sound mind, willfully and voluntarily state my desire that my dying may not be artificially prolonged under the circumstances set forth below:

1. If I have an incurable injury or illness certified to be a terminal condition by two physicians who have personally examined me, one of whom is my attending physician, and if the physicians have determined that there can be no recovery whether or not life—sustaining procedures are utilized because the application of life—sustaining procedures would serve only to prolong artificially the dying process, I direct that life—sustaining procedures be withheld or withdrawn and that I be permitted to die naturally, with only the administration of medical procedures deemed necessary to alleviate pain. I further direct that nutrition and hydration be withheld or withdrawn when the application of such procedures would serve only to prolong artificially the process of dying.

2. If I am unable to give direction regarding the use of life—sustaining procedures, I intend that my family and physician honor this declaration as the final expression of my legal right to refuse medical or surgical treatment and to accept the consequences of this refusal.

3. If I have been diagnosed as pregnant and my physician knows of this diagnosis, this declaration has no effect during the course of my pregnancy.

I understand this declaration and I am emotionally and mentally competent to make this declaration.

_____
Betty B. Smith

I know the declarant personally and I believe her to be of sound mind. I am not related to the declarant by blood or marriage, and am not entitled to any portion of the declarant's estate under any will of the declarant. I am neither the declarant's attending physician nor an employee of the attending physician or of the inpatient health care facility in which the declarant may be a patient and I have no claim against the declarant's estate at this time.

_____
Jerome L. Hollingsworth

_____
Elizabeth S. Hollingsworth

PROOF OF DECLARATION

We, Betty B. Smith, Jerome L. Hollingsworth and Elizabeth S. Hollingsworth, the declarant and the witnesses, respectively, whose names are signed to the foregoing instrument, having been sworn, declared to the undersigned officer that the declarant, in the presence of witnesses, signed the instrument as her intended declaration, that the declarant signed for herself and that each of the witnesses, in the presence of the declarant and in the presence of each other, signed as a witness.

_____
Betty B. Smith

_____
Jerome L. Hollingsworth

_____
Elizabeth S. Hollingsworth

STATE OF FLORIDA
COLLIER COUNTY   ss

Subscribed and sworn to before me on December 7, 1991, by Betty B. Smith, the declarant, who produced her driver's license as identification, and by Jerome L. Hollingsworth and Elizabeth S. Hollingsworth, the witnesses.

_____
Angie C. Badenski, Notary Public
State of Florida at Large
Commission No. AA 753552
My commission expires 2/26/94

(NOTARY SEAL)

This Instrument Prepared By:
Jerome L. Hollingsworth
Attorney at Law
Post Office Box 8124
Naples, FL 33941 – 8124
(813) 263-3773

POWER OF ATTORNEY FOR MEDICAL CARE

Know All Men by these Presents, that I, Alfred A. Smith, 123 Lover's Lane, Naples, FL 33940, Collier County, Florida, have made, constituted and appointed and by these presents do make, constitute and appoint Betty B. Smith my true and lawful attorney, for me in my name, place and stead under the following circumstances:

In the event that I am adjudicated to be incompetent, or in the event that I am not adjudicated incompetent, but by reason of illness or mental or physical disability am, in the opinion of two physicians, unable to properly handle my own affairs, as evidenced by an affidavit or affidavits, copies of which shall suffice, then and in that event, Betty B. Smith shall be my true and lawful attorney, for me in my name, place and stead to do the following:

To contract for, authorize and permit any and all medical, surgical or dental care and administration of medicine, including surgical amputations, hospitalization and placement in a convalescent or nursing home which I may require and which my wife shall deem necessary for me during the existence of this power.

I further grant and give unto my attorney in fact full authority to do and perform any and all other acts necessary or incident to the performance and execution of the powers expressly granted in this instrument, with power to do and perform all acts authorized by it as fully to all intents and purposes as I might or could do if I were personally present for the duration of this power, which power shall exist until I specifically terminate it or it is terminated by operation of law.

This durable power of attorney for medical care shall not be affected by disability of the principal except as provided by statute and is granted to my wife under the provisions of the Florida Statutes. It is my intention that my wife have full power to act as my true and lawful attorney even in the event of my disability or incompetency, from whatever cause; and otherwise granting hereby unto my attorney full power and authority to do and perform all and every act and thing whatsoever required and necessary to be done in and about these premises, as fully to all intents and purposes as I might and could if personally present, reserving full power of substitution and revocation, hereby ratifying all that my attorney shall lawfully do or cause to be done as my attorney in fact.

The powers conferred upon my attorney in fact by this instrument may involve the rendering of burdensome decisions and, therefore, my wife may not desire to act under the authority granted by this power. In the alternative, my attorney in fact may desire to obtain judicial approval of any proposed action to be taken with respect to my health and welfare.

A photostatic copy of this Power of Attorney shall serve equally as well and have the same legal significance as the original.

In Witness Whereof, I have set my hand on December 7, 1991.

Jerome L. Hollingsworth	Alfred A. Smith

Angie C. Badenski

STATE OF FLORIDA ss
COLLIER COUNTY

On December 7, 1991, Alfred A. Smith produced a driver's license as identification and acknowledged this instrument, declaring it to be made of his own free will and deed.

(NOTARY SEAL)

Angie C. Badenski, Notary Public
State of Florida at Large
Commission No. AA 753552
My commission expires 2/26/94

This Instrument Prepared By:
Jerome L. Hollingsworth
Attorney at Law
Post Office Box 8124
Naples, FL 33941 – 8124
(813) 263-3773

POWER OF ATTORNEY FOR MEDICAL CARE

Know All Men by these Presents, that I, Betty B. Smith, 123 Lover's Lane, Naples, FL 33940, Collier County, Florida, have made, constituted and appointed and by these presents do make, constitute and appoint Alfred A. Smith my true and lawful attorney, for me in my name, place and stead under the following circumstances:

In the event that I am adjudicated to be incompetent, or in the event that I am not adjudicated incompetent, but by reason of illness or mental or physical disability am, in the opinion of two physicians, unable to properly handle my own affairs, as evidenced by an affidavit or affidavits, copies of which shall suffice, then and in that event, Alfred A. Smith shall be my true and lawful attorney, for me in my name, place and stead to do the following:

To contract for, authorize and permit any and all medical, surgical or dental care and administration of medicine, including surgical amputations, hospitalization and placement in a convalescent or nursing home which I may require and which my husband shall deem necessary for me during the existence of this power.

I further grant and give unto my attorney in fact full authority to do and perform any and all other acts necessary or incident to the performance and execution of the powers expressly granted in this instrument, with power to do and perform all acts authorized by it as fully to all intents and purposes as I might or could do if I were personally present for the duration of this power, which power shall exist until I specifically terminate it or it is terminated by operation of law.

This durable power of attorney for medical care shall not be affected by disability of the principal except as provided by statute and is granted to my husband under the provisions of the Florida Statutes. It is my intention that my husband have full power to act as my true and lawful attorney even in the event of my disability or incompetency, from whatever cause; and otherwise granting hereby unto my attorney full power and authority to do and perform all and every act and thing whatsoever required and necessary to be done in and about these premises, as fully to all intents and purposes as I might and could if personally present, reserving full power of substitution and revocation, hereby ratifying all that my attorney shall lawfully do or cause to be done as my attorney in fact.

The powers conferred upon my attorney in fact by this instrument may involve the rendering of burdensome decisions and, therefore, my husband may not desire to act under the authority granted by this power. In the alternative, my attorney in fact may desire to obtain judicial approval of any proposed action to be taken with respect to my health and welfare.

A photostatic copy of this Power of Attorney shall serve equally as well and have the same legal significance as the original.

In Witness Whereof, I have set my hand on December 7, 1991.

_____	_____
Jerome L. Hollingsworth	Betty B. Smith

_____
Angie C. Badenski

STATE OF FLORIDA
COLLIER COUNTY ss

On December 7, 1991, Betty B. Smith produced a driver's license as identification and acknowledged this instrument, declaring it to be made of her own free will and deed.

_____
Angie C. Badenski, Notary Public
State of Florida at Large
My commission expires 2/26/94

(NOTARY SEAL)

This Instrument Prepared By:
Jerome L. Hollingsworth
Attorney at Law
Post Office Box 8124
Naples, FL 33941 – 8124
(813) 263-3773

POWER OF ATTORNEY FOR MEDICAL CARE

Know All Men by these Presents, that I, Alfred A. Smith, 123 Lover's Lane, Naples, FL 33940, Collier County, Florida, have made, constituted and appointed and by these presents do make, constitute and appoint Charles C. Smith my true and lawful attorney, for me in my name, place and stead under the following circumstances:

In the event that I am adjudicated to be incompetent, or in the event that I am not adjudicated incompetent, but by reason of illness or mental or physical disability am, in the opinion of two physicians, unable to properly handle my own affairs, as evidenced by an affidavit or affidavits, copies of which shall suffice, and in the event that my wife, Betty B. Smith, is deceased or also adjudicated to be incompetent, or in the event that she is not adjudicated incompetent, but by reason of illness or mental or physical disability is, in the opinion of two physicians, unable to properly handle her own affairs, as evidenced by an affidavit or affidavits, copies of which shall suffice, then and in that event, Charles C. Smith shall be my true and lawful attorney, for me in my name, place and stead to do the following:

To contract for, authorize and permit any and all medical, surgical or dental care and administration of medicine, including surgical amputations, hospitalization and placement in a convalescent or nursing home which I may require and which Charles C. Smith shall deem necessary for me during the existence of this power.

I further grant and give unto my attorney in fact full authority to do and perform any and all other acts necessary or incident to the performance and execution of the powers expressly granted in this instrument, with power to do and perform all acts authorized by it as fully to all intents and purposes as I might or could do if I were personally present for the duration of this power, which power shall exist until I specifically terminate it or it is terminated by operation of law.

This durable power of attorney for medical care shall not be affected by disability of the principal except as provided by statute and is granted to my son under the provisions of the Florida Statutes. It is my intention that my son have full power to act as my true and lawful attorney even in the event of my disability or incompetency, from whatever cause; and otherwise granting hereby unto my attorney full power and authority to do and perform all and every act and thing whatsoever required and necessary to be done in and about these premises, as fully to all intents and purposes as I might and could if personally present, reserving full power of substitution and revocation, hereby ratifying all that my attorney shall lawfully do or cause to be done as my attorney in fact.

The powers conferred upon my attorney in fact by this instrument may involve the rendering of burdensome decisions and, therefore, my son may not desire to act under the authority granted by this power. In the alternative, my attorney in fact may desire to obtain judicial approval of any proposed action to be taken with respect to my health and welfare.

A photostatic copy of this Power of Attorney shall serve equally as well and have the same legal significance as the original.

In Witness Whereof, I have set my hand on December 7, 1991.

_____   _____
Jerome L. Hollingsworth   Alfred A. Smith

_____
Angie C. Badenski

STATE OF FLORIDA   ss
COLLIER COUNTY

On December 7, 1991, Alfred A. Smith produced a driver's license as identification and acknowledged this instrument, declaring it to be made of his own free will and deed.

_____

(NOTARY SEAL)

Angie C. Badenski, Notary Public
State of Florida at Large
My commission expires 2/26/94

This Instrument Prepared By:
Jerome L. Hollingsworth
Attorney at Law
Post Office Box 8124
Naples, FL 33941 – 8124
(813) 263-3773

POWER OF ATTORNEY FOR MEDICAL CARE

Know All Men by these Presents, that I, Betty B. Smith, 123 Lover's Lane, Naples, FL 33940, Collier County, Florida, have made, constituted and appointed and by these presents do make, constitute and appoint Charles C. Smith my true and lawful attorney, for me in my name, place and stead under the following circumstances:

In the event that I am adjudicated to be incompetent, or in the event that I am not adjudicated incompetent, but by reason of illness or mental or physical disability am, in the opinion of two physicians, unable to properly handle my own affairs, as evidenced by an affidavit or affidavits, copies of which shall suffice, and in the event that my husband, Alfred A. Smith, is deceased or also adjudicated to be incompetent, or in the event that he is not adjudicated incompetent, but by reason of illness or mental or physical disability is, in the opinion of two physicians, unable to properly handle his own affairs, as evidenced by an affidavit or affidavits, copies of which shall suffice, then and in that event, Charles C. Smith shall be my true and lawful attorney, for me in my name, place and stead to do the following:

To contract for, authorize and permit any and all medical, surgical or dental care and administration of medicine, including surgical amputations, hospitalization and placement in a convalescent or nursing home which I may require and which Charles C. Smith shall deem necessary for me during the existence of this power.

I further grant and give unto my attorney in fact full authority to do and perform any and all other acts necessary or incident to the performance and execution of the powers expressly granted in this instrument, with power to do and perform all acts authorized by it as fully to all intents and purposes as I might or could do if I were personally present for the duration of this power, which power shall exist until I specifically terminate it or it is terminated by operation of law.

This durable power of attorney for medical care shall not be affected by disability of the principal except as provided by statute and is granted to my son under the provisions of the Florida Statutes. It is my intention that my son have full power to act as my true and lawful attorney even in the event of my disability or incompetency, from whatever cause; and otherwise granting hereby unto my attorney full power and authority to do and perform all and every act and thing whatsoever required and necessary to be done in and about these premises, as fully to all intents and purposes as I might and could if personally present, reserving full power of substitution and revocation, hereby ratifying all that my attorney shall lawfully do or cause to be done as my attorney in fact.

The powers conferred upon my attorney in fact by this instrument may involve the rendering of burdensome decisions and, therefore, my son may not desire to act under the authority granted by this power. In the alternative, my attorney in fact may desire to obtain judicial approval of any proposed action to be taken with respect to my health and welfare.

A photostatic copy of this Power of Attorney shall serve equally as well and have the same legal significance as the original.

In Witness Whereof, I have set my hand on December 7, 1991.

Jerome L. Hollingsworth	Betty B. Smith

Angie C. Badenski

STATE OF FLORIDA ss
COLLIER COUNTY

On December 7, 1991, Betty B. Smith produced a driver's license as identification and acknowledged this instrument, declaring it to be made of her own free will and deed.

_____

Angie C. Badenski, Notary Public

(NOTARY SEAL)

State of Florida at Large

Commission No. AA 753552

My commission expires 2/26/94

This Instrument Prepared By:
Jerome L. Hollingsworth
Attorney at Law
Post Office Box 8124
Naples, FL 33941 – 8124
(813) 263-3773

DURABLE POWER OF ATTORNEY

Know All Men by these Presents, that I, Alfred A. Smith, 123 Lover's Lane, Naples, FL 33940, Collier County, Florida, have made, constituted and appointed and by these presents do make, constitute and appoint Betty B. Smith my true and lawful attorney, for me in my name, place and stead under the following circumstances:

In the event that I am adjudicated to be incompetent, or in the event that I am not adjudicated incompetent, but by reason of illness or mental or physical disability am, in the opinion of two physicians, unable to properly handle my own affairs, as evidenced by an affidavit or affidavits, copies of which shall suffice, then and in that event, Betty B. Smith shall be my true and lawful attorney, for me in my name, place and stead to do the following:

To make, receive, sign, endorse, execute, acknowledge, deliver and possess such applications, contracts, agreements, options, covenants, conveyances of real or personal property, security agreements, bills of sale, leases, mortgages, assignments, insurance policies, documents of title, bills, bonds, debentures, checks, drafts, notes, stock certificates, proxies, warrants, commercial paper, receipts, withdrawal receipts and deposit instruments relating to accounts or deposits in, or certificates of deposit of, banks, savings and loan or other institutions or associations, proofs of loss, evidences of debts, releases and such other instruments in writing of whatever kind and nature as may be necessary or proper in the exercise of the rights and powers herein granted;

This durable family power of attorney shall not be affected by disability of the principal except as provided by statute and is granted to my spouse under the provisions of Section 709.08 of the Florida Statutes. It is my intention that my spouse have full power to act as my true and lawful attorney even in the event of my disability or incompetency, from whatever cause; and otherwise granting hereby unto my attorney full power and authority to do and perform all and every act and thing whatsoever required and necessary to be done in and about these premises, as fully to all intents and purposes as I might and could if personally present, reserving full power of substitution and revocation, hereby ratifying all that my attorney shall lawfully do or cause to be done as my attorney in fact.

A photostatic copy of this Power of Attorney shall serve equally as well and have the same legal significance as the original.

In Witness Whereof, I have set my hand on December 7, 1991.

_____   _____
Jerome L. Hollingsworth   Alfred A. Smith

_____
Angie C. Badenski

STATE OF FLORIDA
COLLIER COUNTY   ss

On December 7, 1991, Alfred A. Smith produced a driver's license as identification and acknowledged this instrument, declaring it to be made of his own free will and deed.

_____

(NOTARY SEAL)

Angie C. Badenski, Notary Public
State of Florida at Large
Commission No. AA 753552
My commission expires 2/26/94

This Instrument Prepared By:
Jerome L. Hollingsworth
Attorney at Law
Post Office Box 8124
Naples, FL 33941 – 8124
(813) 263–3773

DURABLE POWER OF ATTORNEY

Know All Men by these Presents, that I, Betty B. Smith, 123 Lover's Lane, Naples, FL 33940, Collier County, Florida, have made, constituted and appointed and by these presents do make, constitute and appoint Alfred A. Smith my true and lawful attorney, for me in my name, place and stead under the following circumstances:

In the event that I am adjudicated to be incompetent, or in the event that I am not adjudicated incompetent, but by reason of illness or mental or physical disability am, in the opinion of two physicians, unable to properly handle my own affairs, as evidenced by an affidavit or affidavits, copies of which shall suffice, then and in that event, Alfred A. Smith shall be my true and lawful attorney, for me in my name, place and stead to do the following:

To make, receive, sign, endorse, execute, acknowledge, deliver and possess such applications, contracts, agreements, options, covenants, conveyances of real or personal property, security agreements, bills of sale, leases, mortgages, assignments, insurance policies, documents of title, bills, bonds, debentures, checks, drafts, notes, stock certificates, proxies, warrants, commercial paper, receipts, withdrawal receipts and deposit instruments relating to accounts or deposits in, or certificates of deposit of, banks, savings and loan or other institutions or associations, proofs of loss, evidences of debts, releases and such other instruments in writing of whatever kind and nature as may be necessary or proper in the exercise of the rights and powers herein granted;

This durable family power of attorney shall not be affected by disability of the principal except as provided by statute and is granted to my spouse under the provisions of Section 709.08 of the Florida Statutes. It is my intention that my spouse have full power to act as my true and lawful attorney even in the event of my disability or incompetency, from whatever cause; and otherwise granting hereby unto my attorney full power and authority to do and perform all and every act and thing whatsoever required and necessary to be done in and about these premises, as fully to all intents and purposes as I might and could if personally present, reserving full power of substitution and revocation, hereby ratifying all that my attorney shall lawfully do or cause to be done as my attorney in fact.

A photostatic copy of this Power of Attorney shall serve equally as well and have the same legal significance as the original.

In Witness Whereof, I have set my hand on December 7, 1991.

_____   _____
Jerome L. Hollingsworth   Betty B. Smith

_____
Angie C. Badenski

STATE OF FLORIDA   ss
COLLIER COUNTY

On December 7, 1991, Betty B. Smith produced a driver's license as identification and acknowledged this instrument, declaring it to be made of her own free will and deed.

_____
Angie C. Badenski, Notary Public
State of Florida at Large
Commission No. AA 753552
My commission expires 2/26/94

(NOTARY SEAL)

This Instrument Prepared By:
Jerome L. Hollingsworth
Attorney at Law
Post Office Box 8124
Naples, FL 33941 – 8124
(813) 263–3773

DURABLE POWER OF ATTORNEY

Know All Men by these Presents, that I, Alfred A. Smith, 123 Lover's Lane, Naples, FL 33940, Collier County, Florida, have made, constituted and appointed and by these presents do make, constitute and appoint SunBank/Naples, NA my true and lawful attorney, for me in my name, place and stead under the following circumstances:

SunBank/Naples, NA is the successor trustee of a funded living trust between Alfred A. Smith and Betty B. Smith as settlors and Alfred A. Smith and Betty B. Smith as trustees. It is our intention to transfer all of our assets into this trust. This power of attorney is drawn for the purpose of giving our successor trustee the power to transfer assets into our trust which are outside our trust.

In the event that I am adjudicated to be incompetent, or in the event that I am not adjudicated incompetent, but by reason of illness or mental or physical disability am, in the opinion of two physicians, unable to properly handle my own affairs, as evidenced by an affidavit or affidavits, copies of which shall suffice, and in the event that my wife, Betty B. Smith, is deceased or also adjudicated to be incompetent, or in the event that she is not adjudicated incompetent, but by reason of illness or mental or physical disability is, in the opinion of two physicians, unable to properly handle her own affairs, as evidenced by an affidavit or affidavits, copies of which shall suffice, then and in that event, SunBank/Naples, NA shall be my true and lawful attorney, for me in my name, place and stead to do the following:

To make, receive, sign, endorse, execute, acknowledge, deliver and possess such applications, contracts, agreements, options, covenants, conveyances of real or personal property, security agreements, bills of sale, leases, mortgages, assignments, insurance policies, documents of title, bills, bonds, debentures, checks, drafts, notes, stock certificates, proxies, warrants, commercial paper, receipts, withdrawal receipts and deposit instruments relating to accounts or deposits in, or certificates of deposit of, banks, savings and loan or other institutions or associations, proofs of loss, evidences of debts, releases and such other instruments in writing of whatever kind and nature as may be necessary or proper in the exercise of the rights and powers herein granted;

This durable power of attorney shall not be affected by disability of the principal except as provided by statute and is granted to my successor trustee under the provisions of the Florida Statutes. It is my intention that my successor trustee have full power to act as my true and lawful attorney even in the event of my disability or incompetency, from whatever cause; and otherwise granting hereby unto my attorney full power and authority to do and perform all and every act and thing whatsoever required and necessary to be done in and about these premises, as fully to all intents and purposes as I might and could if personally present, reserving full power of substitution and revocation, hereby ratifying all that my attorney shall lawfully do or cause to be done as my attorney in fact.

A photostatic copy of this Power of Attorney shall serve equally as well and have the same legal significance as the original.

In Witness Whereof, I have set my hand on December 7, 1991.

_____   _____
Jerome L. Hollingsworth   Alfred A. Smith

_____
Angie C. Badenski

STATE OF FLORIDA
COLLIER COUNTY   ss

On December 7, 1991, Alfred A. Smith produced a driver's license as identification and acknowledged this instrument, declaring it to be made of his own free will and deed.

_____
Angie C. Badenski, Notary Public
State of Florida at Large
Commission No. AA 753552
My commission expires 2/26/94

(NOTARY SEAL)

This Instrument Prepared By:
Jerome L. Hollingsworth
Attorney at Law
Post Office Box 8124
Naples, FL 33941 – 8124
(813) 263–3773

DURABLE POWER OF ATTORNEY

Know All Men by these Presents, that I, Betty B. Smith, 123 Lover's Lane, Naples, FL 33940, Collier County, Florida, have made, constituted and appointed and by these presents do make, constitute and appoint SunBank/Naples, NA my true and lawful attorney, for me in my name, place and stead under the following circumstances:

SunBank/Naples, NA is the successor trustee of a funded living trust between Alfred A. Smith and Betty B. Smith as settlors and Alfred A. Smith and Betty B. Smith as trustees. It is our intention to transfer all of our assets into this trust. This power of attorney is drawn for the purpose of giving our successor trustee the power to transfer assets into our trust which are outside our trust.

In the event that I am adjudicated to be incompetent, or in the event that I am not adjudicated incompetent, but by reason of illness or mental or physical disability am, in the opinion of two physicians, unable to properly handle my own affairs, as evidenced by an affidavit or affidavits, copies of which shall suffice, and in the event that my husband, Alfred A. Smith, is deceased or also adjudicated to be incompetent, or in the event that he is not adjudicated incompetent, but by reason of illness or mental or physical disability is, in the opinion of two physicians, unable to properly handle his own affairs, as evidenced by an affidavit or affidavits, copies of which shall suffice, then and in that event, SunBank/Naples, NA shall be my true and lawful attorney, for me in my name, place and stead to do the following:

To make, receive, sign, endorse, execute, acknowledge, deliver and possess such applications, contracts, agreements, options, covenants, conveyances of real or personal property, security agreements, bills of sale, leases, mortgages, assignments, insurance policies, documents of title, bills, bonds, debentures, checks, drafts, notes, stock certificates, proxies, warrants, commercial paper, receipts, withdrawal receipts and deposit instruments relating to accounts or deposits in, or certificates of deposit of, banks, savings and loan or other institutions or associations, proofs of loss, evidences of debts, releases and such other instruments in writing of whatever kind and nature as may be necessary or proper in the exercise of the rights and powers herein granted;

This durable power of attorney shall not be affected by disability of the principal except as provided by statute and is granted to my successor trustee under the provisions of the Florida Statutes. It is my intention that my successor trustee have full power to act as my true and lawful attorney even in the event of my disability or incompetency, from whatever cause; and otherwise granting hereby unto my attorney full power and authority to do and perform all and every act and thing whatsoever required and necessary to be done in and about these premises, as fully to all intents and purposes as I might and could if personally present, reserving full power of substitution and revocation, hereby ratifying all that my attorney shall lawfully do or cause to be done as my attorney in fact.

A photostatic copy of this Power of Attorney shall serve equally as well and have the same legal significance as the original.

In Witness Whereof, I have set my hand on December 7, 1991.

_____   _____
Jerome L. Hollingsworth   Betty B. Smith

_____
Angie C. Badenski

STATE OF FLORIDA
COLLIER COUNTY   ss

On December 7, 1991, Betty B. Smith produced a driver's license as identification and acknowledged this instrument, declaring it to be made of her own free will and deed.

                                    _____
                                    Angie C. Badenski, Notary Public
(NOTARY SEAL)   State of Florida at Large
                                    My commission expires 2/26/94

This Instrument Prepared By:
Jerome L. Hollingsworth
Attorney at Law
Post Office Box 8124
Naples, FL 33941 – 8124
(813) 263–3773

JEROME L. HOLLINGSWORTH

Attorney at Law

Licensed in Florida

Michigan & Wisconsin

2500 Tamiami Trail North, Suite 221

Naples, Fl. 33940 *

(813) 263 - 3773

December 7, 1991

To: **WHOM IT MAY CONCERN**

Re: Taxation of The Alfred and Betty Smith Living Trust

Prior to January 1, 1981, all trusts were tax paying entities, and the trustee of any trust was required to obtain an employee identification number for the trust and to report any income with respect to the trust property on FORM 1041. However, since that date, the trustees of a "grantor trust" neither apply for an employee identification number nor report trust income on FORM 1041. Instead, the beneficiaries report the income on their FORM 1040. A grantor trust is a trust where the settlors remain the effective owner of the trust property and at least one settlor is either a trustee or co-trustee.

CONCLUSION

1. Alfred A. Smith and Betty B. Smith must provide their social security numbers to payers of income with respect to property in their living trust and need not obtain an employer identification number for their living trust.

2. Alfred A. Smith and Betty B. Smith do not file FORM 1041, but report any income with respect to trust property on their FORM 1040.

I reach these conclusions for the reasons specified below:

IDENTIFYING NUMBERS AND INCOME TAX RETURNS

Income Tax Regulation 301.6109 defines the numbers under which tax-payers identify themselves for income tax purposes. This regulation reads, in pertinent part, as follows:

> (a) <u>In general</u>
> (1) <u>Social security numbers and employer identi-fication numbers.</u> There are two types of taxpayer iden-tifying numbers: social security numbers and employer identification numbers. Social security numbers take the form 000-00-0000, while employer identification num-bers take the form 00-000000. Social security numbers identify individual persons and estates of decedents . . . .

* * *

165

(2) <u>Certain grantor trusts.</u> A grantor trust described in Reg. 1.671–4(b) shall not obtain an employer identification number until such time as the trust is no longer described in Reg. 1.671–4(b). Instead, the grantor of such a trust must furnish his or her social security number (or, when applicable, his or her employer identification number) to payers of income, and payees must report income as if paid to the grantor, not the trust.

(b) <u>Use of one's own number.</u> Every person who files under this title a return, statement, or other document shall furnish his taxpayer identifying number as required by the forms and the instructions relating thereto. A person whose number must be included on a document filed by another person shall give the taxpayer identifying number so required to the other person on request. * * *

Income Tax Regulation 1.671–4 not only determines whether the settlors or grantors of a trust need to apply for an employer identification number, but also determines whether or not the settlors or grantors need to file FORM 1041. This regulation reads, in pertinent part, as follows:

(b) <u>Trust income taxed entirely to grantor.</u>

(1) In the case of a trust when

(i) the same individual is both grantor and trustee (or co-trustee), and

(ii) that individual is treated as owner for the taxable year of all of the assets of the trust by the application of section 676,

a FORM 1041 should not be filed. Instead, all items of income, deduction, and credit from the trust should be reported on the individual's FORM 1040 in accordance with its instructions. For provisions dealing with taxpayer identifying numbers, see Reg. 301.6109–1 (Regulations on Procedure and Administration).

(2) In the case of a trust when

(i) a husband and wife are the sole grantors, and

(ii) one spouse is trustee or co-trustee with a third party or both spouses are trustees or co-trustees with a third party, and . . . .

         (iii) one or both spouses are treated as owners of all of the assets of the trust for the taxable year by the application of section 676, and

         (iv) the husband and wife for the taxable year make a single return jointly of income taxes under section 6013,
a FORM 1041 should not be filed. Instead all items of income, deduction, and credit from the trust should be reported on the spouses' FORM 1040 in accordance with its instructions.

         (3) This paragraph (b) of the section shall not apply to a trust if the situs of the trust or any of the assets of the trust are not in the United States.

The question of whether or not the trustees need to file for an employer identification number for the trust and whether or not the income with respect to the property in the trust is taxed to the settlors or grantors of the trust is resolved generally by the application of a two pronged test. The first prong requires the settlor (or at least one of the settlors of a joint trust) to be a trustee or a co-trustee. The opening paragraph of The Alfred and Betty Smith Living Trust as it stands presently contains the proper provision and reads, in pertinent part, as follows:

         Agreement made December 7, 1991, between Alfred A. Smith and Betty B. Smith (the "Settlors"), Alfred A. Smith and Betty B. Smith (the "Trustees") and SunBank/Naples, NA (the "Successor Trustee").

The second prong of the test requires the settlors or grantors to have reserved the power to revoke as defined in IRC Section 676. This section reads, in pertinent part, as follows:

         (a) GENERAL RULE. The grantor shall be treated as the owner of any portion of a trust, whether or not he is treated as such owner under any other provision of this part, where at any time the power to revest in the grantor title to such portion is exercisable by the grantor or a nonadverse party, or both.

Alfred A. Smith and Betty B. Smith reserved the appropriate power of revocation in their trust agreement. That agreement reads, in pertinent part, as follows:

ARTICLE IV
Settlors' Power to Amend and Revoke

The Settlors may, during their lifetimes: (1) withdraw property from this Trust in any amount and at any time upon giving reasonable notice in writing to the Trustees; (2) add other property to the Trust; (3) change the beneficiaries, their respective shares and the plan of distribution; (4) amend this Trust Agreement in any other respect; (5) revoke this Trust in its entirety or any provision of it; provided, however, the duties or responsibilities of the Trustees shall not be enlarged without the Trustees' consent nor without satisfactory adjustment of the Trustees' compensation.

Alfred A. Smith and Betty B. Smith are trustees as required by Reg. 1.671-4, and Alfred A. Smith and Betty B. Smith reserved the Power to Revoke as defined under IRC Section 676. Alfred A. Smith and Betty B. Smith need not file for an employer identification number for the trust nor file FORM 1041 to report income with respect to property in the trust.

However, after the death of Alfred A. Smith and Betty B. Smith, or in the event that they should become legally incompetent so as to make the trust irrevocable, the trustee will be required to apply for an employer identification number for the trust and file FORM 1041 to report income with respect to property in the trust.

Please direct any requests for further information concerning these matters to our office.

Very truly yours,

Jerome L. Hollingsworth

JLH/acb

JEROME L. HOLLINGSWORTH

Attorney at Law

Licensed in Florida

Michigan & Wisconsin

2500 Tamiami Trail North, Suite 221

Naples, Fl. 33940 *

(813) 263 - 3773

December 7, 1991

Alfred A. Smith and Betty B. Smith
123 Lover's Lane
Naples, FL 33940

Re: Transfers to The Alfred and Betty Smith Living Trust

Dear Alfred and Betty:

You must understand that although a Living Trust and a Pourover Will provide an excellent mechanism for management during lifetime, avoidance of death taxes and provision for the passing of assets from a deceased to others without protracted probate, they are nothing more than tools. If you do not use these tools, they will be of no benefit to you.

You must also understand that these tools will not do tax planning for you. You must decide how the assets are to be managed and how they are to go to those who are the objects of your affection. The documents, themselves, provide you with no tax planning whatsoever.

In this letter, I shall explain how you go about transferring assets to the trust.

1. Common or Preferred Stocks Held in Your Own Names. (Your stock broker or your bank can transfer these for you. If you wish to do this yourself, proceed as follows.)

    a. The name of the <u>transfer agent</u> is on the stock certificate.

    b. Write a letter to the transfer agent telling him how you want the stock to be registered.

    c. The registration should read, "Alfred A. Smith and Betty B. Smith, Trustees of the Alfred and Betty Smith Living Trust dated December 7, 1991".

    d. You must inform the transfer agent of the social security numbers of the life beneficiaries of the trust (your social security numbers).

169

e. You must also tell the transfer agent where you want the dividends and proxies mailed (mailing address of Trustees – 123 Lover's Lane, Naples, FL 33940).

f. You should then sign the back of the certificates as "assignor", leaving blank the person to whom you assign them.

g. Procure a <u>signature guarantee</u> from a bank or stock broker.

h. Send all of the above by registered mail, return receipt requested, to the transfer agent.

Note: Be certain you know what your cost basis is in the stock.

2. Bonds Held in Your Own Names

a. Registered bonds are treated the same as stocks.

b. Bearer bonds should be reduced to registered form.

Note: If you decide to keep bonds in bearer form, keep them in an envelope marked so that anyone will know that the contents of the envelope belong to the trust and note that these bonds are part of the trust on Schedule A.

3. Real Estate

a. Prepare and record deeds transferring real estate and any interest you may have in land contracts or mortgages to "Alfred A. Smith and Betty B. Smith, Trustees of the Alfred and Betty Smith Living Trust dated December 7, 1991".

b. You may wish to treat your home or your part time home differently. If you do, remember two things:

(1) Anything which is titled will have to be probated if it is not in the trust or in joint ownership.

(2) Schemes of joint ownership will only avoid probate if you die before the person with whom you own the property jointly.

4. Notes Due From Others – Endorse the back of the note specifically to "Alfred A. Smith and Betty B. Smith, Trustees of the Alfred and Betty Smith Living Trust dated December 7, 1991".

5. Checking & Savings Accounts.

    a. Make joint checking and savings accounts payable on death to "SunBank/Naples, NA, Trustee of the Alfred and Betty Smith Living Trust dated December 7, 1991".

    b. The names on the signature card can be whatever is convenient to the settlors.

Note: The checks need not reflect the fact that this account is payable on death to a trustee and can show only the settlors' names.

6. Life Insurance

    a. You can avoid any death taxes on life insurance by giving up <u>all incidents of ownership</u> to the death beneficiary. Do this through the mechanism of a separate life insurance trust. If death taxes are not so great a problem as management of the death proceeds from life insurance, name the death beneficiary as follows:

    b. For insurance on the life of Alfred A. Smith, make the prime beneficiary "Betty B. Smith, Trustee of the Alfred and Betty Smith Living Trust dated December 7, 1991", and the alternate beneficiary "SunBank/Naples, NA, Trustee of the Alfred and Betty Smith Living Trust dated December 7, 1991".

    c. For insurance on the life of Betty B. Smith, make the prime beneficiary "Alfred A. Smith, Trustee of the Alfred and Betty Smith Living Trust dated December 7, 1991", and the alternate beneficiary "SunBank/Naples, NA, Trustee of the Alfred and Betty Smith Living Trust dated December 7, 1991".

Note: The beneficiaries of life insurance policies must consent in writing to any change. The insurance agent will know how to do this.

7. IRA – Make the named beneficiaries the same as for life insurance, unless you wish to give your spouse the power to roll the IRA over into an IRA for your spouse. In such a case, make your spouse the prime beneficiary and the trustee the secondary beneficiary of the IRA.

8. A trust can have important tax planning possibilities. Show this letter and the trusts agreements to the person who does the taxes. If you have been doing your own taxes, seek the advice of an accountant and discuss the tax possibilities of the trusts.

9. The investment portfolio, other than investments in closely held businesses, which is being handled by a broker should be put in the name of the trustee. Show this letter to the broker and they will make the necessary adjustments to the account and make a proper accounting to the trust.

10. Sometimes, a person with whom you are dealing with respect to the trust will want to see what authority the trustee has. In such a case, give the person a copy of the Certificate of Trust Existence and Authority. This certificate shows who set up the trust, names the trustees and explains their succession and tells what powers the trustees have with respect to property which is in the trust.

Very truly yours,

Jerome L. Hollingsworth

JLH/acb

Index

H. I. SONNY BLOCH *is an author, lecturer, and broadcaster whose daily and weekly radio shows (including "The Sonny Bloch Show" and "Today's Business Journal") air on WOR in New York and 150 stations throughout the U.S. He lives in New York and Florida. Jerome L. Hollingsworth is an attorney specializing in estate and tax planning. He lives in Florida.*

SONNY BLOCH'S

Cover Your Assets